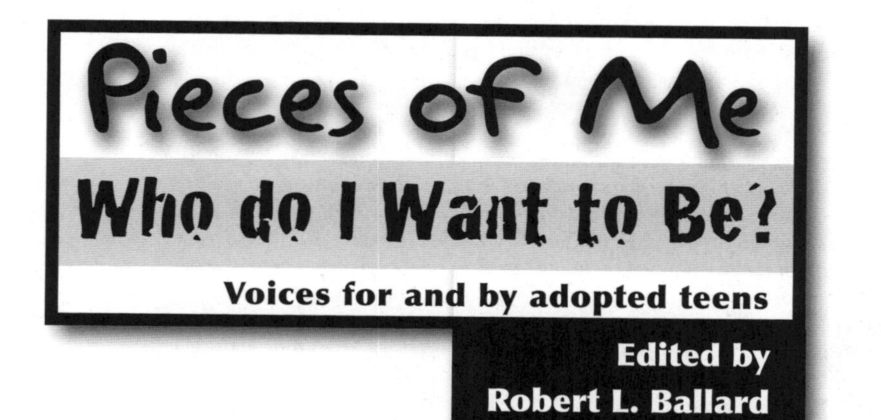

EMK Press • Warren, New Jersey

EMK Press, a subsidiary of EMK Group, LLC
16 Mt. Bethel Road, #219
Warren, NJ 07059
www.emkpress.com

Publisher's Cataloging in Publication data
Ballard, Robert L.
Pieces of me, who do I want to be? / edited by Robert L. Ballard.
p. cm.
Summary: A book for adopted and fostered teens that offers healing, help, and hope as they find, understand, and embrace the pieces that make up who they are.
ISBN 9780972624442

1. Adopted children. 2. Teenagers--Psychology. 3. Adoptive parents. 4. Adoption--Psychological aspects. 5. Adopted children--Family relationships. I. Title.

HV875.55 .B35 2009
649/.145--dc22 2009934542

Manufactured in the United States of America

09 10 11 12 13 14 15 16

Cover and interior design by Carrie Kitze
The typeface on the cover is called "Akbar" and was created by Jon Bernhardt. It can be downloaded for free at www.wobblymusic.com/groening/akbar.html

Pieces of Me
Who do I Want to Be?

I tell you this story because
for too many years,
people have told
my stories for me.
I am ready
to speak for myself.
So where do I begin?

juli jeong martin

This collection is dedicated in the spirit of Ned Levy
and the many other adoptees, young and old, who
seek to transform the world for the better
through the expression of their voice –
in story, music, art, poetry, and body.

Ned's story can be found on page 79.

Table of Contents

Gathering the Pieces 5-38

Stolen Pieces 39-76

Fitting the Pieces 77-110

Sharing the Pieces 111-136

Where do These Pieces Go? 137–160

The Journey is only Begining 161

Ways to Connect 163

With Thanks . . .

This book is a special one to me as it touches on issues close to my heart and life. However, a project like this one involves more than one person, and I am indebted to these wonderful people for their personal and professional contributions to this book:

Chi-Ying Jan, who kept Carrie and me organized and pointed in the right direction. I don't know how she does it.

Sheena Macrae, who was one of the original visionaries of the book and its first editor. I took over knowing she had already done so much. This book would not be possible without her.

Carrie Kitze, who invited me to become a part of the project, guided me along the way, and is a pleasure to work with. Carrie is wise, generous, insightful, smart, and grounded. I could not ask for a better publisher or a better friend.

Adria and Kyla, my two daughters, who have helped me gather my own pieces and be proud of what I share.

Sarah Ballard, my life partner and, in many ways, a co-editor of this collection. This book could not have happened without her support, perspective, and ideas. More than anyone, she has helped me figure out my own pieces. While I still struggle fitting my pieces together, words cannot express my gratitude and love for her.

Most importantly, I need to acknowledge all of the authors, artists, musicians, organizations, and families who submitted to this project. I wish each and every submission could have been in this book. It was a pleasure and joy to read them all, and everyone who submitted should take heart in knowing they have affected at least one adoptee with their expressions.

Finally, my son in Vietnam, who I am still waiting for as I write this. He is my personal inspiration for this book. When this book was stressful or I wasn't sure how I was going to complete it, I would imagine how this book would offer him something I did not have as an adoptee growing up – knowing that he is not alone.

Robert L. "Bert" Ballard
Editor

It's a jigsaw puzzle.

Either you brought it home from the store or you found it hiding in a closet. Either way, you want to put it together because the picture is amazing or it just looks like fun. Or, more likely, you have nothing better to do. What do you do first? Where do you begin?

Of course, first you would open the box.
But then what?

Would you pour all of the pieces onto the floor or table? Would you keep them in the box? Would you turn the picture over to make it more of a challenge or would you want the picture as a guide? Would you find all of the edge pieces first, with their one flat side? Or do you group all of same patterns and colors together?

Do you find the corners first? Or do you figure out the brightest pattern and put those together? Do you invite others to help and partake? Or do you like the challenge of doing it by yourself? Is this for fun and enjoyment? Or are you trying to beat a personal best time?

By now you should have figured out that there are many ways to put a puzzle together, that there is no one best strategy. But no matter what way you approach it – edges first, by yourself, with the picture, on a table, on the floor – the goal is the same – complete the puzzle!

Life as an adopted teenager is kind of like a puzzle. There's this picture of who you want to be, but you're not quite sure how the pieces fit. And you're not sure where to begin.

You have some pieces that you know and others you don't. You have some pieces you want to find, but don't know how. You have some pieces you wish you didn't have. And you have some pieces that you're not sure how they fit or why they're even there.

How do you begin putting together the Pieces of Me, those pieces and parts of your life that make up who you are and who you want to be? Where do you start? Who do you talk to? What

do you need to be most concerned about?

No doubt there are a lot of people who are giving you advice. (One of them may have even given you this book hoping it'll help you out.) But, really, their advice just doesn't make sense sometimes. You don't need more advice; what you need is to know that whatever you're doing to figure out your pieces is just fine.

Remember the puzzle you were trying to put together? Remember the goal? The idea is to find ways for the pieces to fit, and there is no one, best way to put a puzzle together.

That is why we – and many others from around the world – put this book together. We want you to know that there are many ways to put the puzzle of who you are together, there are many ways to fit your pieces together. And only you can figure it out.

In this book are the voices of others like you, others trying to figure out where their pieces go. Some have come a long way; others are just

It is the same with Pieces of Me – there is no one, best way to put the puzzle of who you are and who you want to be together. In fact, there are many, many ways.

beginning. There are voices and expressions of adoptive parents and adult adoptees. There are perspectives from adoption professionals and adoptive families.

But most importantly, there are voices just like your own – adoptive teenagers who are from different countries, look different than their families, have experienced the foster care system, have reunited with birth families, have returned to birth culture, enjoy being adopted, hate being adopted, have been abused, have loving families, own pets, do art, love music, like to travel, have career goals, have no idea who they want to be, have children, never want to have kids . . . well, you get the idea.

They are just people . . . people who are adopted and are trying to figure out where their pieces fit.

We've broken the book into five basic sections, relating to your adoption journey and relating to puzzles. There's Gathering the Pieces, those pieces that we're trying to find and connect with. There's Stolen Pieces, those pieces of ourselves that have been taken away from us. There's Fitting the Pieces, those pieces that, though challenging, we've figured out where they go. There's Sharing the Pieces, when who we are meets the rest of the world, sometimes with success and sometimes with disaster. And there's Where Do These Pieces Go?, those pieces that you just have no idea what to do with.

It's like putting a jigsaw puzzle together. Except that it's not, because it is about figuring out the pieces of you.

And, like a real-life puzzle, this book doesn't have one best way to read it. You can start at the beginning and read to the end. You can read from the end to the beginning. You can start in the middle. You can read a story one day and a poem the next. You can try one of the activities to help you figure it out or you can express yourself on one of the blank pages . . or any of the pages for that matter – it's your book!

If one day you're struggling, you can read about Stolen Pieces and be comforted by others' voices. If on another day you are down, you can read Sharing the Pieces to find inspiration. If on another day, you are excited because you figured out a part of you, you can read Fitting the Pieces and know you are not alone. If on another day you miss your birthparents, you can read Gathering Pieces and find out what others have discovered on their journeys of connection.

It doesn't matter how you read it, and it doesn't matter how you fit your pieces. It just matters that you are working toward figuring it, for yourself.

Oh, by the way, I'm 34 years old, and I'm an adoptee, too. I was adopted from Vietnam in 1975 as part of Operation Babylift (look it up on Wikipedia or join a group on Facebook to find out more). I was supposedly born in Saigon (now Ho Chi Minh City, Vietnam). I was supposedly at an orphanage called "An Lac," meaning "Happy Place." My first name was someone else's – "Vu Tien Do II." I'm 34 years old, and I still don't know what the "II" means exactly. Today, I am called Bert even though my official name is Robert.

Everyday I try to figure out the pieces to my puzzle. Everyday I try to figure which pieces I need to gather, which pieces were stolen, which ones how to fit them, how to share them, and what to do with a whole lot of pieces that are just there waiting to find a place.

With all of the voices that grace these pages, maybe we can figure it out together. Maybe we can realize that we're not so alone and that others are on the same journey. Maybe we can take some steps to figuring out our own way of putting together the puzzle of our lives. Maybe we can even share some of our pieces with one another.

Remember when you opened the box and you saw all the pieces to the jigsaw puzzle? And then you wondered what to do next – dump them out or keep them in the box? Sort them by edges or by pattern? You were trying to figure out how to gather the pieces so you could put the puzzle together.

This book is as much for me as it is for you. I'm still trying to figure it out, too, just like you are.

It's the same with our lives as adopted persons. We are trying to gather the pieces so we can put them together. We're trying to reconnect with birth family or birth country. We're trying to find a friend or role model. We're trying to find ourselves. We're trying to relate to our adoptive family or adoptive community. We're trying to understand the importance of blood ties or birthmarks.

Open the box. Turn the page. Let's find the Pieces of Me: Who do I want to be?

We're showing how it doesn't have to make sense for it to be connected. We're showing how gathering pieces helped us see our puzzle in new and revealing ways. This book tells these stories. With art, poem, and passion, many have and are still trying to gather those pieces to figure out where they fit into our personal puzzles of who we are and who we want to be.

Robert "Bert" Ballard
Editor,
Adoptee, Husband, Father
Summer 2009

Gathering the Pieces

Remember when you opened the box and you saw all the pieces to the jigsaw puzzle? And then you wondered what to do next – dump them out or keep them in the box? Sort them by edges or by pattern? You were trying to figure out how to gather the pieces so you could put the puzzle together.

It's the same with our lives as adopted persons. We are trying to gather the pieces so we can put them together. We're trying to reconnect with birth family or birth country. We're trying to find a friend or role model. We're trying to find ourselves. We're trying to relate to our adoptive family or adoptive community. We're trying to understand the importance of blood ties or birthmarks.

We're showing how it doesn't have to make sense for it to be connected. We're showing how gathering pieces helped us see our puzzle in new and revealing ways. This section tells these stories. With stories, art, poem, and passion, many have and are still trying to gather those pieces to figure out where they fit into our personal puzzles of who we are and who we want to be.

My Birthmark: Finding My Real Family

By Gerard Wozek

Growing up, I was often teased because of an oddly shaped, dark brown blemish that floats just below my navel. "Is that where the stork bit you?" I would sometimes hear my peers shouting out at me. "Is that where you're growing another bellybutton or did you spill some ink near your waistline?"

Even though the discolored blotch was only about the size of a quarter, the imperfection felt immense to me as an adolescent as well as throughout most of my teen years. It was so large in my mind that I never liked to go shirtless in public. At the beach, at the community swimming pool, even after gym class, when all the other boys were stripped down for their locker room showers, I'd wear my undershirt pulled down securely over this congenital skin anomaly.

"It's just a birthmark," my high school best friend and next-door neighbor Edward would often remind me in a consoling manner. "If you don't make a such big deal about it, then no one else will."

It was a clear hereditary link to a family I grew up never knowing.

But it was a big deal to me. It was a clear hereditary link to a family I grew up never knowing. It was the mark created at birth that identified me as part of a unique and particular tribe—a blood related brood that I would never be able to locate because of the strict privacy laws in place during the time of my closed adoption that permanently sealed my birth records.

"See now this is where they cut the umbilical cord to my biological mother," I remember pointing out to Edward one day as we lay in our connecting backyards with our sixteen-year-old bellies exposed to the summer sun one afternoon. "And right underneath is the 'mother-spot' that connects me to my real mom, the woman who carried me for nine months only to give me up to the Catholic Charities, she is the woman I can never begin to imagine or really know as my real family."

The Dutch word "moedervlekken," or "mother-spots," refers to a birthmark that an infant supposedly inherits solely from the mother. It is also claimed that the birthmark is a result of a mother's unfulfilled hopes and unrequited desires.

"So supposedly, you're carrying all your biological mother's disappointed wishes with you then?" Edward said after a long while scrutinizing my uneven nevus in the stark sunlight.

"Yes," I responded. "And maybe the biggest regret was that she never got to know me. She never had the chance to see me grow up or had the opportunities to influence or plant in me the kinds of ideas and life lessons that she would have hoped to."

I often fantasized about meeting my biological mother. I would imagine walking in a crowd of strangers, and suddenly out of the corner of my eye, I would see a striking birthmark on a woman's forearm or neck or ankle that would match my own completely. Then I would look into her eyes and instantly recognize her as being the mother who was unable to keep me and raise me as her own child.

For a long while growing up, I found myself actually examining people for conspicuous birthmarks that were similar to my own. I remember even asking my freshman composition teacher in high school if the spot under her earlobe was a mole or a beauty mark because it looked so identical to mine. Her initial response was a somewhat bewildered and flushed look that indicated perhaps I was being a bit too intrusive.

But my whole life I've struggled to locate the obvious and identifiable attributes in others that might somehow connect me to them as family. In each of the close, biological families I knew of growing up, I was always able to discern a distinguishing physical or emotional feature that was prominent—a characteristic that would connect all of the clan members together. So it would make sense that as a teenager, I would seek out those noticeable familial traits in others that would suggest just exactly where I belonged. Whether it was a birthmark, or similar facial features, or a particular gait or disposition that corresponded to my own, I have always been searching for my true relations in the world.

However, my journey as an adoptee has led me to discover that what I've actually been doing all along is redefining and reinterpreting the notion of what exactly a family truly is. A family isn't necessarily the one you are biologically connected to, or even and especially not the family that you physically might resemble the most. The fact of the matter is, as adoptees, we choose our families—not because the other individuals favor us through some identifiable characteristic or even share our individual tastes and proclivities. Rather, our selected families are comprised of a mutual understanding of what is most important in life. This coordination of values and sympathies extends beyond physical and mental aspects and goes to what is at the very core of our being.

The fact of the matter is, as adoptees, we choose our families...

I have met my real brother and my real sister and my real mother and my real father in the most uncommon of places. No, this chosen family does not share my bloodline or my experiences of childhood or even my eye-catching birthmark. But my selected family is as authentic and as genuine as any biological family that I know. We share a bond that connects us on the deepest of levels—as well as real-life struggles, misunderstandings, and disappointments as any related group does. Together, we enjoy the kind of understanding and shared values that I would hope for in any group of individuals that calls themselves a family: mutual respect, absolute trust, tempered patience, and unflinching honesty.

If birthmarks really are unfulfilled wishes then that is what binds me to my biological mother. It is also what I have learned to accept as part of who I am—a complex portrait of someone who was delivered into the arms of another family from a mother who undoubtedly did have dreams and wishes for me. I'm certain, however, that one of her wishes has been fulfilled, the wish that I could locate a family that would care for me and love me in the most authentic of ways. Those are the qualities that make up the family that I have discovered—the family that I have chosen to be part of my life.

That summer day long ago when my buddy Edward was scanning the imperfection just below my navel, he remarked that perhaps there might be another way of looking at my birthmark—another way in which I could interpret this small blemish which at the time felt so prominent to me.

"Maybe your birthmark isn't a symbol of a hopeless wish," he said, "Maybe this is where your real mom kissed you as an infant, maybe this is where she pressed her lips as you were released into the world. And this permanent mark is your biological mother's way of letting you know that she is like your guardian angel, always with you, right next to your umbilicus—the place where you were forever separated from her body."

After that revelation, I began to slowly lose my shame and embarrassment for my birthmark. I've come to understand that I was carried for nine months, and somehow really loved completely through that experience and beyond it. I know that I carry my birthmother's kiss wherever I go, a tangible, physical symbol of her devotion and concern, as I continue to look for her indelible spirit in the faces of everyone I meet.

Gerard Wozek teaches English and the humanities at Robert Morris University Illinois in Chicago. His first book of poetry, "Dervish," won the Gival Press Poetry Award. He is currently working on a creative memoir surrounding his experiences growing up in a closed adoption.

"You can't teach anybody anything, only make them realize the answers are already inside them."
Galileo

The Dance by Stacy K. Pearson

This piece was created as a love letter to my biological parents. In a way, it was a message across the entire unknown of all of the questions and all of the pain. It was to share that I have always felt them, their connection with me, how I am a part of them, how our lives are forever bound...in an eternal dance. Find Stacy's other art on pages 18, 49, 52, 101, and 151.

My Search, My Lessons

by Jena Leddon

At fourteen, I thought that I knew everything I wanted out of my life: I wanted to be a journalist, I wanted to fall in love, get married, have a family, and I wanted to be reunited with my biological family.

At fifteen, I started corresponding with my birthmother through letters, via a liaison (in my case, an aunt would receive them and forward them to my mother). I came to expect these letters every two weeks and I would be quite happy when they came. I looked forward to my biological mother's words, pictures, stories of growing up. I looked forward to hearing her remind me that she loved me for me.

Eventually, after nearly a year of writing back and forth, my mom agreed that I could meet with my birthmother. On a school night, we met at a mall that's located about forty-five minutes away from where I live. It was busy and chaotic and stressful, but my mom left us alone to talk in the food court. Two hours later, she came back and I realized that I hadn't spent nearly enough time with her. We had talked endlessly, laughing at my nervous habits and exchanging stories of my half-siblings.

At our next face-to-face meeting, my birthmother brought with her some interesting news. She had contacted my birthfather, who I also had questions about. I had no idea how I really felt about him and his (lack of) involvement in my adoption; I just wanted details to put to my story, a name, a face, an age – whatever! I just wanted something that connected me to her, me to him, and them to each other.

When she contacted him, he was surprised to say the least. He hadn't heard from her in sixteen years and he was surprised to hear her voice over the phone line. He had married and had children of his own. There was two thousand miles of distance between us, but he wanted to get to know me... if that's what I wanted.

I wrestled with the idea for about two hours after I left her company that evening. Finally, I sat down and penned out my first letter to him. I sent it and waited. A week went by and I panicked. I e-mailed him and he responded that he "anxiously awaited" my letter. Three or four weeks after that one line e-mail, I received a response in the mail (this time, it was mailed to my birthmother, then to my aunt and then to me).

We e-mail on occasion, but not often enough to amount to a "healthy relationship," in my opinion. Over the past two years, I've received less than fifty e-mails and sometimes it's hard to remind myself that he has his own life now that is full of boy scouts, baseball games, working, being a good husband, father, son… and that he doesn't have as much room for me as I'd like. It's been an internal struggle as I've wrestled with the thought of sending him that fateful e-mail or letter that says that I can't do this anymore until I learn to understand patience more.

I still haven't sent that e-mail or letter. I've still never heard his voice say my name. His kids know about me, but with the distance, it seems like a dream that we'd ever even meet. Sometimes I think I like that probability; I can imagine in my head that they don't exist and I'm his. Mostly, I don't let my dreams get that far-fetched.

At eighteen, I have learned a lot more than I ever thought I would: about the world, relationships, matters of blood, and signatures placed on legally binding documents.

As much as I believe that reuniting myself with my biological family has helped me grow into the young woman I am today, I can also acknowledge the fact that it sometimes has hurt me. I sometimes find myself wanting more than letters, e-mails or phone calls. I sometimes find myself mad at my adoptive family, although I have no right to be mad at them. Sometimes I find myself mad at my biological family for a whole host of reasons that they had no stake in.

They say that hindsight is twenty-twenty. They say that blood is thicker than water. With my understanding of my own adoption, I wouldn't change one single experience – good or bad. I'll take the extra stress and emotions over not knowing any day. When it boils down to it, my biological family has just as much to do with who I am today as does the family I grew up with.

Jena Leddon is a 19 year-old college student from Western Pennsylvania. She hopes that her story highlights the trials and tribulations of any reunion and offers hope to those searching.

Finding My Mother, Finding Myself

By Sheena McFarland

I'm talking with my birthmother.
She's almost exactly as tall as I am, and she and I share the same shape of eye and mouth. She laughs with the same bubbling giggle as I do. She opens her mouth to share another amusing story from her childhood . . .

"Ma'am, what beverage would you like tonight?"

The flight attendant interrupts my day dreams. I'm only three hours into my 17-hour flight to Mumbai, and I can't stop thinking about what I would do if I found my birth-mother.

What would I say to her? Would she be happy to see me? What would she say to me?

And then the voice inside my head starts telling me that it doesn't matter if I meet my birthmother. I can't expect to hop on a plane, travel halfway around the world and magically meet the woman who gave birth to me nearly 25 years ago.

There's the part of me that desperately wants to see if my birthmother and I really do share faces. I want to know what part of my personality comes from her (or her mother or her father) and what part my parents shaped.

I want to ask her why she gave me up. I want to know if she thinks of me. I want to know what life would have been like had I stayed.

I also don't want an answer to those questions. No matter what she says, would it be a good enough reason to justify her abandoning me? If she does think of me, do I want to know someone is out there, pining away for a daughter she'll never know? And do I really want to know how my life would have been so incredibly different had I been raised in India, as opposed to Utah?

Those thoughts torture me throughout the plane ride, making my heart beat faster and harder than during any 5K I've run.

I meet my aunt Karen in Mumbai, and it's nice to see a familiar face, a face of someone I love. Her face is reminiscent of her sister, my mother, who's back home in Utah. My aunt keeps my head clear and my goals focused: I'm here to find a piece of myself that has been missing since I can remember. The piece of me that tells me the story of my first six weeks of life, the piece that tells me the story of my face.

We board a train to the state of Goa, to the city of Panaji, where I was born.

I stare out the small, rain-drenched window, looking at the lush, green ravines of seemingly never-ending jungle. I picture what my birthtown must look like.

In my mind, it's a city of tropical beaches, Hindu temples and children running around–the children who were doomed to the streets instead of being adopted.

Instead, what I see as I get off the train shocks me: Panaji is a Catholic tourist town.

Thanks to my Birthmother on my Birthday

By Shefalie Chandra

Mother,
It is my birthday
And I think of you...
Thank you, for my life...
In all the passing years
I still think of you.
This day... My day...
Not much celebration going on
The day you delivered me.
But oh, my mother...if you could see me now...
I would want it to bless your heart...
To see what I have done with the gift of life given to me.
I am so sorry you could not keep me or
Watch me grow and bloom into the woman
I am becoming today.
I am sorry it was not your hand that held me
As a child in the night when I was so afraid.
Nor your voice that comforted me in the darkness and challenges of my life...
Nor your laughter or your encouragement I heard
Throughout my youthful growing years.
You have not seen the many places, and people
Whose lives have touched me and I them, and all
That has gone into making me...Me.
I remember you and smile.
But still...here I am...
I am trying to do the best with my life I can.
I have loved, laughed, climbed mountains,
Walked in the valleys and....well, sometimes
I have even stopped to rest in the shadows for oh so long...
Until I had almost forgotten the warmth of the sun.
I am learning to let people into my life and heart
And build a bridge to friendship.
I have known times of deep loss, but also the pleasure of much gain...
And I have known the joy of being raised with a family.
I have been a daughter...and a sister...a wife...a mother...
And a friend to many who have lost their way in life...
I so wanted you to meet my friends...
I wanted you to meet the woman who became my "mum."
I am learning to sing in the barren times, and the times of plenty...
I am learning to let the light shine from within...
And to let the wounds heal over...
I am learning to sing a new song.....
And I wanted to say thank you.
I think of you and wanted you to know
My life has gone on...
And I am coming into full bloom...
And this day of all days... my birthday,
I remember you and smile.

Shefalie Chandra is an adoptee of dual heritage living in the UK. She is involved in helping disadvantaged people overcome life's challenges to grow and develop. About her poem, she says, "It expresses words I couldn't say for years... how hard it was to get to where my adoption and teen years made some sense and I felt ok about myself. I hope it says something to you, too. Don't give up!"

Western-style churches line the streets, all the buildings have a Portuguese flair and signs advertising hotel, restaurant, and beachfront specials fill the streets.

This is not the India I was anticipating. Where is the bustle and poverty and beauty of Delhi? Where is the never-ending stream of autorickshaws? Where is the smell of freshly slaughtered chickens or freshly caught crabs? What is this sanitized version of India I never knew existed?

I swallow hard and try to fight back the disappointment. I've always had a hard time telling people I'm from India, as I don't share its culture, but now I feel like I've truly been deceiving people. This city isn't India. It's the generic resort town that could be found anywhere in the world.

That piece of me that I've been missing for so long feels farther away from me than ever before. That piece of me now feels like a lie.

That piece of me that I've been missing for so long feels farther away from me than ever before. That piece of me now feels like a lie.

I try to shake off that feeling, and start the hunt for my orphanage.

As I walk through the streets, I gaze more intently at the strangers passing me than I normally would. Are those my eyes? Are those my cheekbones? What about that nose? It looks a lot like mine. But am I just trying too hard?

I know it's foolish, but I secretly hope someone will point at me and shout: "You look just like my cousin or sister or aunt."

It doesn't happen. Instead, I get into an autorickshaw with my aunt, and start the short drive to the area I'm from.

I have the Panaji neighborhood name of Caranzalem, but the address I have isn't quite complete. I spend hours in an autorickshaw, looking. The driver keeps getting out, asking people if we are getting close. As time passes, the frustration builds. Even the sound of the tide crashing into shore does nothing to soothe me. Suddenly, I realize how hot and sticky I feel, and I tell the driver to take us back to the hotel.

After further research, I find out the orphanage doesn't exist anymore. It closed years ago.

I lose it.

I lock myself in the bathroom and the tears start falling. I've traveled halfway across the world to find a place that no longer exists.

That voice inside my head starts piping up: What did you expect? You're being naive. And why do you care so much? A year ago, you hadn't even given a moment's thought to your orphanage, and now you're sobbing that it's gone.

But it's more than the loss of a place; it's a loss of myself. The shuttering of that orphanage closed off any hope of finding someone who might have remembered me or my birthfamily.

The loud honking of trucks and cars in the road screams through the bathroom window, bringing me back to reality. Though I'm devastated, the tears stop and I join my aunt for dinner.

At breakfast the next morning, a headline in the newspaper makes my aunt hand the pages over to me. Apparently, all of the birth certificates in the area had recently been moved to this city. Getting a copy of that had never occurred to me, but now it seems like the most obvious action.

I still have that voice in my head, doubting if I'll find anything, but I wend my way through the streets of Panaji, passing shopping malls, medical clinics and dodging the various vehicles seemingly trying to run me down in the street.

I walk up the stairs of a dingy building, often catching whiffs of the ammonia-laden smell I can identify but don't want to think about. On the third floor, I write down my birthname, Natasha Barboza, and my birthdate, Sept. 19, 1982, and hand it to a woman sitting in front of a computer. She types for about five minutes, looks up, and tells me she has the record. It will take about an hour to obtain.

The next hour passes in a whirl of rainclouds, cacophony and overly buttery food.

When I finally go back, they can't find who has the copy. That's when my aunt calls to me from across the room, holding a small rectangle of paper. There it is, my birthmother's name: Maria Barboza.

It feels like the whole world goes quiet. I no longer hear the people in the hallway bickering in Hindi. The smell of ink and paper fades. I have it. I have proof that I really did exist in this city at some point.

It's that piece of paper that I take out of my money belt throughout the rest of my trip, just to look at it.

It has its own significance, but it's also just one of a dozen other souvenirs I'm bringing home with me from India. I came looking for my birthmother and ended up with a piece of paper. Had someone asked me if that would have been enough before I left for India, I would have said, "No."

Now it is enough.

I'm happy knowing where I came from, but I realize I'm happy too with the life I've led since my first six weeks. I have a family who loves me unconditionally; I have dear friends and a career I'm thrilled with.

The pieces of my life I've always known about are enough to make me whole.

Even though none of the faces I gazed into on the streets of Goa had my eyes, my nose or my lips, I realize I finally found the face I was looking for: my own.

Sheena McFarland is a 27-year-old Indian adoptee from Centerville, UT. Her story about "Finding My Mother, Finding Myself" came out of a trip to India in 2007 to research her roots. Sheena wrote about her experience for The Salt Lake Tribune, where this article originally appeared.

Do you think you're ready to search for your birthfamily?
Do you think you've thought it through? Not even sure what questions to ask yourself? Hollee McGinnis, Korean adoptee, social worker, and policy director for the Evan B. Donaldson Adoption Institute (www.adoptioninstitute.org), has come up with 10 "Moment of Truth" questions every adoptee should ask when thinking about searching for birth family and birthparents. To find out more about these questions and ask them of yourself, go to www.holtintl.org/adoptees/mcginnis.shtml

by Grace

(names have been changed to respect everyone's privacy)

I grew up with a vague idea of my birthparent's history so I always knew that there were reasons they weren't able to be my parents. I knew that both my parents had problems with drugs and alcohol and had spent time in institutions. This information has had a great impact on me growing up. Was there more to them than just the list of issues? For me, learning about my birthparent's history was something difficult but necessary in figuring out who I am.

I was born in July 1982, and for nine days was cared for by my mother in a hospital. After a couple of weeks, I was placed in a foster home. When I was nine months old, I went to live with the couple who became my adoptive parents. At a relatively young age, I had access to my file. There was part of me that wanted to wait until I was older, maybe married with my own family, and settled into a job. However, I felt that in order for me to get on with my life, the past was something I had to deal with. I am so glad that I went ahead with it, although it is only now that I realize how difficult it was for me at the time.

I already knew some things that my Mum had told me when I was younger. I had a vague idea about most of the information, but seeing it in black and white for the first time was still very painful. My birthparents' background included mental health issues, periods spent in institutions, drug and alcohol abuse. My mother in particular had a very unhappy childhood. She witnessed her fathers' violence towards her mother and was placed in foster care herself. She later went on to attempt suicide and suffered from alcoholism, schizophrenia, personality disorders, anorexia, the list goes on. These were largely triggered by her unhappy childhood and drug abuse. At the time, when I was reading the words, they seemed to go over my head. It was almost as if it was happening to someone else.

I am not at all advocating that this kind of information be withheld in order to protect adoptees. I feel strongly that no matter how bad the reality, you need to be told the truth. Most adoptees instinctively have an idea about the circumstances surrounding their adoption; often, the truth is never as bad as you imagine.

When I found out about my birthparents' background, it had a negative impact on me. I wondered if perhaps I was going down the same path they did. I found the information given in my file, and the way it was presented, quite distressing to read. It just seemed like an endless list of negatives, and gave me the impression that both my parents had always led wretched, tragic lives. Because they are my parents and I have feelings for them, this made me very sad. What did this say about me as a person? I wondered if maybe this was the reason why my life didn't seem to be working out the way that other people's did. Both my birthparents had suffered so much and had so many problems. It was as though I was predestined to be unhappy, never to find my way in life, no matter how hard I tried. I realize now that I was being irrational, but I couldn't tell myself that at the time.

Several years after reading my file, my birthfather got in contact with my social worker, asking for information about me. My social worker asked my Mum if she would be willing to send a letter and some photos every six months to my birthfather and she agreed. He also sent me letters that were forwarded to me by my social worker. My Mum was very sympathetic towards my birthfather. She said he would love to meet me one day, and she would be right behind me if I wanted to. I just never felt ready. Although I was pleased that my birthfather had gotten in touch, it stirred up a lot of emotions that I wasn't ready to face.

I never stopped thinking about my past, and especially had thoughts about my birthmother. My birthmother's sister was friendly with my birthfather and she wrote me a letter through my social worker. At the age of nineteen, I decided that I would like to meet my aunt. The meeting went well, and I continued to write to her and to my birthfather. After some time, I felt ready to meet him, too.

It is just hard to meet a stranger who is part of oneself, because it feels so strange and unfamiliar...

Our one meeting went really well, and I have very fond memories of the afternoon that we spent together. However, I did find certain aspects of the meeting difficult. It was obvious that my birthfather was a particularly kind, gentle and caring man, who had so much concern for me, and regrets about the past. He died less than a year after we met. I feel very sad that I never got the chance to see him a second time. We kept in contact by letter, and were gradually getting to know each other, but our relationship never really progressed beyond that. It is very difficult for me to admit, but I do think that knowing what I did about his past problems with drugs and alcohol (about which he was very open), and his resulting mental health issues acted as a barrier between us. It is just hard to meet a stranger who is part of you, because it feels so strange and unfamiliar. This was especially true because I was at a stage in my life when my self-confidence, grounding, and direction were all rather shaky.

After we met, I felt both positive and negative things because I could never really shake the feelings of sadness about what happened in the past. Meeting someone after twenty-three years can't make up for that. You can't get those years back or reverse the things that have happened to people. I didn't blame him, or feel any kind of rejection or anger. I just felt sad about the whole thing in general, even though I have had such a happy childhood with my adoptive family. My birthfather was able to tell me some positive things about my birthmother as well and I have clung to the smallest details: the music she liked, why she chose my name, the time she went to his parents' house for dinner, even that she liked handbags and shoes. These tiny pieces of information all help to make her a real person, and detract from the horror I felt when I read about the personal tragedy she had suffered and everything else she went through. I couldn't help but feel some of the pain she must have felt.

I went to my birthfather's funeral, which was quite daunting, but something I felt I really had to do. I had already met two of his sisters and an aunt, and I was beginning to have more of an idea of who he was as a person, and what his life was like before his problems began. I began to see beyond his 'problems' for the man he really was. The funeral itself was obviously very upsetting for me. However, going to his funeral and meeting his friends, allowed me more of an insight into his life and made me feel much more positive about everything. After the service finished, I met some of my birthfather's friends from his Alcoholics Anonymous group.

When I met other people from the meetings, I realized that they had been very good friends with my birthfather and they had been a very important part of his life. They all had so many good things to say about him; stories to tell, things they used to do together, etc. I also couldn't believe how much warmth and affection they showed me, and how pleased they were to meet me. It was almost as if they were my family. The best thing was that they knew everything that had happened. My birthfather had told them about my being adopted and why, but none of it seemed to matter anymore. There were no secrets; there was nothing to hide. It was a relief to be with

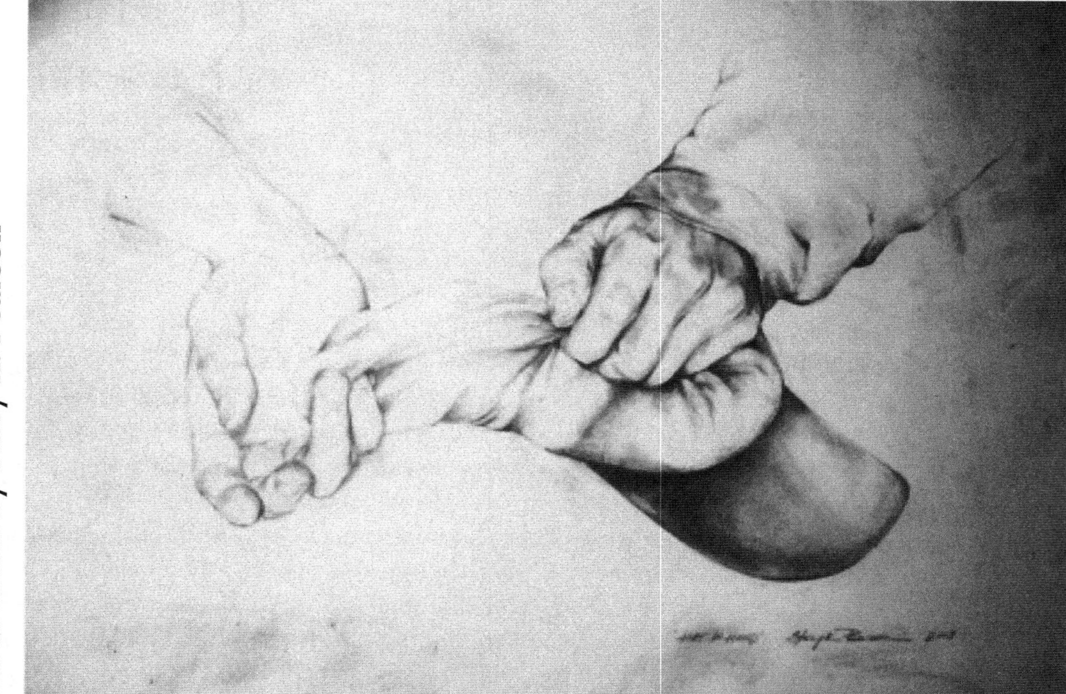

Hat in Hand by Stacy K. Pearson

This is by far my favorite of the pieces in this collection. I made this for my biological father whom I found in April of 2008 after many, many years of searching. It was a gift for our first Father's Day together. "Hat in Hand" signifies how we came to one another.....with only what we had in our hearts: openness, honesty, and vulnerability. When I think of this drawing, I think about how much my father loved me from the very first moment we made contact. In every mark of the pencil I gave back to him my love, hopes, joy, and (hopefully) the healing that he brought to my heart. Find Stacy's other art on pages 9, 49, 52, 101, and 151.

people who knew what had happened, accepted it, and didn't judge me.

What meant so much to me was that they helped me to realize the whole person that my birthfather really was. His horrible list of problems in my adoption file–the substance abuse, mental health issues, long-term unemployment–became a small part of the whole person. He was a man who had lived a varied life, which had touched many other people. It made me so happy. It was as if a weight had been lifted off my shoulders. The card that they gave me, which everyone had signed to say how much that they missed him, will always mean so much to me.

I also went to the scattering of my birthfather's ashes and met two of his friends from childhood who hadn't been able to come to the funeral. I had to chance to listen to their stories and memories of him, how they all used to go traveling together around Europe and America, and the fun they used to have. This was really important to hear because it helped me to get an idea of what he was really like as a person. They sent me some photos of when they were all in their teens and these mean a lot to me.

I know I could have gotten to know my birthfather better if we had been able to meet again. But it is hard when two 'strangers' meet, knowing so little about each other. It is hard to know where to start getting to know one other–there are no etiquette books. I think it takes a while to get over the initial strangeness of meeting for the first time. I just feel sad that I didn't have the chance to get to know him properly in the short time that we had. Many people don't understand how much love and what strong bonds there are between children and their adoptive parents and this should be emphasized despite all of the difficulties. But despite this, I don't think adoption should be seen as a 'magic wand' that can be used to erase the past. No matter how much you are loved by your adoptive parents, your birthparents will always be an important part of who you are.

Today, I am feeling a lot more positive about my adoption. I have more confidence and the problems that my birthparents had no longer seem to be so important. I have learned to accept them and see them as just one part of the many things that made my birthparents who they were. This is largely the result of meeting friends and family of my birthfather who have told me so much about him. Sadly, I have not yet had any positive experience like this from anyone connected with my birthmother. I have met my aunt, but she does not talk about her sister very freely, and that is understandable because they both had difficult childhoods, and spent much time apart, both being placed in foster care after the death of their mother. I do feel better knowing that in the brief relationship she and my birthfather had must have been a happy time for both of them. I hope that she had friends who cared for her too and to whom she was close –like my birthfather's friends from the AA group. The sad thing is I will never know...

'Grace' is a twenty-six year old adoptee from London, England. She wrote 'Grace's Story' while coming to terms with meeting her birthfather and his subsequent death. She is currently studying medicine and has recently been able to contact some friends of her birthmother who would like to meet her someday. See her poem "Looking for Mary" on page 42.

Search for Connections

By Jennifer Arndt-Johns

My parents' response to my questions about my adoption always left me feeling empty. I never doubted my adoptive parents loved me. Their love was obvious. I have experienced it throughout my life in a multitude of ways, and I continue to feel their love for me. They provided me with the only information they had been given from the adoption agency. And the adoption agency had provided them with the only information they had been given. My story, like the stories of thousands of others, is a legacy of unknowns.

What I didn't understand is why the individuals who should have been my biological Korean family abandoned me. The questions are endless. They have taunted me relentlessly throughout my entire life, despite my attempts to silence them. I managed to suppress them for the greater portion of my youth, but my efforts waned as emotional ripples turned into riptides and the riptides turned into a massive waves of emotions that threatened me.

I drowned.

I drowned in sorrow for the loss of my connections to my birthright. I drowned in hate towards the society that would not permit the woman who birthed me to keep me. I drowned in anger because of her inability to stand up for herself and fight to keep her child. I drowned in the envy I felt towards others who were not like me. I drowned in sadness because of the isolation I felt. I drowned in fear because of all that I did not know. For these reasons and many more, I drowned. And when I let it all wash over me, somehow, I surfaced with new understanding.

Understanding myself has not been something that has come easily. In fact, for half of my life I have misunderstood who I am and in return, I have been misunderstood.

I often reflect on what landed me in this complicated predicament. What I have realized is that my identity is full of contradictions. When set within the majority, I am not normal. I have learned to accept and understand this, but getting here hasn't been easy. Further complicating the issue is the fact that when I return to the country of my birth, when set within the majority, I am not normal there either. One can easily see how this might start to make a person a little bit insecure.

In 1996 I returned to South Korea for the first time since my adoption. Here, I met many adopted Koreans who had traveled to the other side of the world seeking the same answers to the same questions I had been asking myself my entire life. Out of this experience I created a documentary, "Crossing Chasms," about the experiences of adult adopted Koreans and their journeys back to their country of birth. Through meeting other individuals who had been adopted from Korea, as well as other countries from around the world, I realized that I was not alone. I also realized that I was as normal as normal can be. If only I had known earlier.

After returning from Korea, I learned about the many social, political and historical events that lead to the beginnings of adoption. This understanding provided me with a sense of where I belonged on the spectrum of Korean adoption. I became involved with artists and activists who were working to galvanize social change in international adoption. These experiences have contributed to what I look back upon as a complete deconstruction of my identity and gradually, piece by piece, like a collage, I have been reconstructing who I am and who I want to become.

The better part of the reconstruction process has been letting go of things that have negatively impacted me. I would like to share something that a dear friend of mine, Marietta Spencer, founder of post-adoption services, shared with me years ago. I met Marietta at the debut of my documentary at the Walker Art Center in 1998.

"You've expressed you were abandoned on the steps of a police station. I am here to let you know you were not abandoned, you were left to be found."

Marietta introduced herself to me after the screening and expressed she would like to keep in touch about my efforts in the field of international adoption. She proceeded to tell me that the story I was told about the beginning of my life was incorrect. I was a bit confused at first, but I listened.

"You've expressed you were abandoned on the steps of a police station. I am here to let you know you were not abandoned, you were left to be found. Whomever was faced with the difficult choice of choosing adoption for you, made sure that you were placed somewhere where you would be found. Abandonment is a word that was created by the social institutions and legal institutions facilitating adoptions, but it should be removed from their terminology. I just wanted you to know that."

I stood stunned for a moment, whacked over the head by a word that had up until that point defined my very existence. I had told my story over and over and over again to people when asked about my adoption, "I was abandoned. ... I was abandoned. ... I was abandoned." I never realized how profoundly negative and damaging that word had been to me until that moment. That evening, I went home and looked up the word in the dictionary.

ABANDONED, adj. 1. forsaken, deserted
2. unrestrained; uncontrolled
3. utterly lacking in moral restraints; shameless.

How could anyone feel good about the circumstances of their adoption when they were "abandoned"? How could anyone feel anything but anger and betrayal by individuals who had "forsaken" and "deserted" their child? But, for the first time I sat and embraced the thoughts that Marietta had shared with me, "You were placed somewhere you would be found." I closed my eyes and imagined for the first time the anguish and heartache that must have enveloped whomever carried me to my destination on that very day. Tears poured down my face as I forgave those who didn't abandon me, but who placed me on those steps with all the hope in the world that I would be found.

> **These experiences have contributed to what I look back upon as a complete deconstruction of my identity and gradually, piece by piece, like a collage, I have been reconstructing who I am and who I want to become.**

Since then, I have learned that thirty-one years ago, I was FOUND on the doorstep of a police station in Milyang, a rural town located outside of Pusan, South Korea. After I was found, officials took me to the local orphanage. My records indicate I was approximately three months old at the time. Because the orphanage did not have the facilities to care for infants, I was transferred to Holt Adoption Agency and three months later, at the age of six months, I was adopted into an American family. This is how my life as an adopted Korean began.

For everyone, life is a continuous journey. But for those who are adopted internationally, we have a few extra steps that we need to take as we strive to create healthy identities for ourselves. Through the communities our families have forged because of adoption and being connected to one another, we can help each other and help others better comprehend our experiences so that we can be understood. We cannot allow ourselves to be defined by others, less we will continue to be misrepresented and misunderstood. May we find strength in our personal histories and be proud of who we are, with all of our intricate complexities and contradictions.

Jennifer Arndt-Johns was adopted from South Korea in 1974. She is a filmmaker, artist/activist and the Founder/Director of Rainbow World, a nonprofit dedicated to creating and distributing educational multimedia about international adoption.

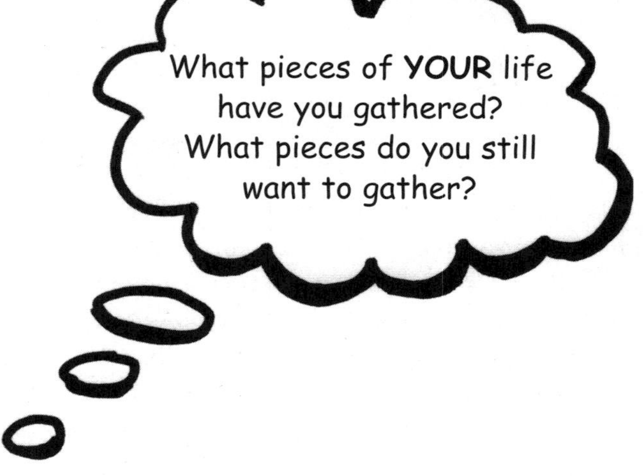

A Little "Brother"

By Jaclyn Champnella

China is a beautiful country where I once lived. I lived there for about four years and then I was adopted into a wonderful family. I took care of a little boy while I lived there who was about two years younger than I was. I cared about him very much. He was like a little brother to me. The year I was adopted I was crying and very sad because I had to leave him at the orphanage by himself.

My mom told my aunt about the little boy I took care of in China. I couldn't stop thinking about him. Then one day my aunt and uncle decided that they were going to adopt Lee. That's the American name my aunt and uncle named him. I was so happy. He was going to be my new cousin. I couldn't wait until I saw him. My mom, aunt, uncle and I all flew to China to get Lee. We had to wait for a couple of days before we could get him, so we visited some sites. We saw the Forbidden City and the Great Wall of China. That was my second time visiting China. I love it there. There are so many beautiful sites to see.

The day my aunt and uncle got my new cousin, I was excited and nervous. When I saw him I gave him a big hug. He means so much to me. Even though he's not really my brother and is my cousin, I am happy as long as I get to visit with him once in a while.

I am hoping that one day I will go back to China and visit my orphanage. I also want to return to the Great Wall of China. Hopefully, that will be soon. I am really fortunate that I was adopted and that my cousins were adopted.

One of the things about being adopted and having taken care of Lee is that I realize how many kids are needy in the world and that we all should try to help them. Many kids are living in a safe home because they were adopted. One day I am hoping to get a lot of money, help the needy, and help more and more kids be adopted. Adopting Lee was one great big change in my life. Now I don't have to worry about him living in China and being by himself.

Jaclyn Champnella is a 14 year-old Chinese adoptee from Farmington Hills, MI. Her story has been told in the book ***The Waiting Child: How the Faith and Love of One Orphan Saved the Life of Another***. In 2003 she became the first child ever awarded the Congressional Coalition "Angel in Adoption" award.

What Real Love Truly Is

by Marisa Cox

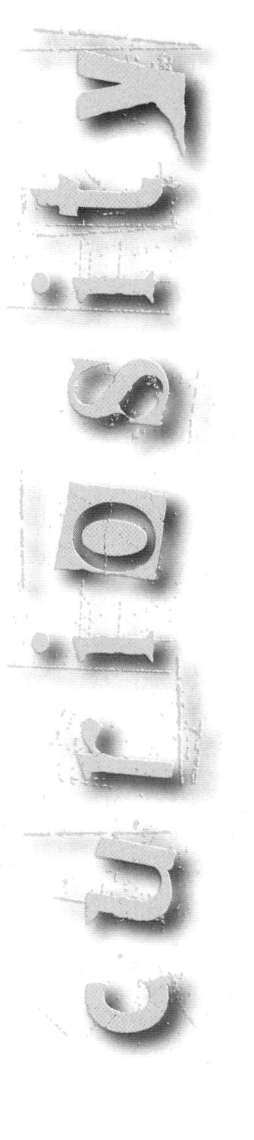

I grew up confused about my adoption. I understood the facts. but I wanted to know more; I was curious. My parents were very understanding about my curiosity and were open to questions, however I knew they didn't have the answers and I didn't want to offend them. Growing up adopted can bring up many complicated emotions. I felt like a part of me was incomplete. Living in the present and preparing for the future is significant, however, I felt the past was an important part of me. Many adoptees (especially teenagers) like me feel that while the present and future is important, our past can help with self-identity and with figuring out who we are.

> I grew up confused about my adoption. I understood the facts. But I wanted to know more.

My life has been eventful from the minute I was born. I was born in Paraguay, a small but beautiful country in South America. I was placed for adoption because my mother couldn't take care of me. She was very young and did not have support at home, so I was secretly placed for adoption. I came to the United States to live with an Irish-American family. They told me about my adoption when I was young, but more importantly they helped me through the phase of non-acceptance. They told me I was adopted when I was in kindergarten, and surprisingly, I understood everything they were saying.

They told me that my mother loved me and that she couldn't take care of me due to the very rough conditions she was in with my biological family. They told me that just because I'm not blood related to them, I am still their daughter. I understood that. However, I wanted to know about my birthmother and why. They had no answers. This confused and upset me. I wasn't really angry with anybody. I was angrier about why there were no answers. My adoptive parents told me where I was from, my biological mother's name, how I got here, what my biological name was, what day I came to the US, when my adoption day was, who my foster mother was, that I have a biological sister who was placed for adoption, my adoption story, and that they loved me.

That's all I knew…that's all they knew.

From time to time I wondered about my biological family. I'd wonder, "Are they ok? Are they in good hands? Are they starving in the streets? Are they homeless? Do they have serious problems? Do they ever think of me? Do they still love me? Does my biological mother think of me on my birthday?" When I felt down sometimes I got angry and upset and thought, "What was my biological mother thinking!?" Or even, "She could have handled me! She must have abandoned me or didn't want me!" Then I'd feel ashamed for such a thought and felt like I was being selfish. I'd then redirect my thinking and tell myself she wanted a better life for me. All of these emotions can be very overwhelming.

When I was seven, I remember one night when I was up late. I cried because I was nervous about where my mother was, where my father was, where my sister was...everything! Did she ever marry someone? Did she have any more kids? Would she ever replace me? Could she be…dead? The last two questions put me in tears. My parents asked me what was going on, but I held back. I finally told them I was having a hard time accepting my adoption. I was amazed at their empathy and kindness. They were incredibly patient through years of confusion and frustration.

I was torn between loyalties for my adoptive parents and my biological parents. I felt ashamed that I loved somebody I didn't even know as much as the people who have raised my for almost my entire life. It felt strange that I loved and missed somebody I didn't even know. I know now that it is not.

> I felt ashamed that I loved somebody I didn't even know just as much as the people who have raised my for almost my entire life

Some adoptees may be afraid to learn about their past because they are scared of what information they will find. It also may be difficult to learn about the conditions that their biological families live in or the history of why they were placed for adoption. Every story is unique but learning about your past can be intimidating at any age. I have felt this way many, many times. I wanted to learn about my biological family but for me it was a blur of complicated feelings.

In August of 2006, I had an opportunity

That is what real love truly is. Always forgiving, ready to support me, making sure I'm getting the right education, making sure I'm healthy, and so much more.

to learn about my birth country when my family took a trip to Paraguay. We went with kids of all different ages and their families. Our group was from all over: the United States, England, and Canada. But we had one thing in common, we were adopted from Paraguay. We could all relate to each other, tour the country, and locate foster and biological families. I was able to reunite with my fostermother, Carmen. She told me about my biological mother and social workers went to search for my biological family. I was ready, but at the same time afraid. I didn't know what I was going to find out. We weren't able to connect with my biological family on this trip.

On April 26, 2007, when I was in the sixth grade, the long journey finally came to an end. I was outside and my father told me to come with him. My parents were waiting with a package. I thought, "Ok, yell at me. What did I do now?" But no, it was a report. It was the most special report I'll ever get in my entire life. They had located my biological family!

When they told me the news the emotions were overwhelming and I broke down in tears of joy. They found wonderful information about them. My questions were answered and even more information was added. I found out what my mother liked to do, what her family was like, where she lived and where my other relatives lived, my father's name and occupation, and so much more. She was alive, she never would replace me and she didn't have any more children. She even said she'd want to have CONTACT with me. I wrote to her on Mother's day. It was amazing. No words can describe it.

I have changed since the day I found my biological parents. I know now that it is normal to have all of the complicated emotions and to have all of those questions, although back then I thought some of them could be bizarre. I am also more aware of the importance of adoption issues and family.

Along with that, I have more appreciation for the life I have been given in the United States. After I've seen how life can be in Paraguay, I am extremely thankful for living in the United States. Paraguay is a gorgeous country with beautiful sunsets, nice rainforests, and wonderful people. However, after seeing the poverty there it made me thankful for living in the United States. Whether somebody is adopted or not we should always be thankful for what we have and not dwell on the what we cannot have.

I am grateful for my adoptive parents, they have gone out of their way to give me a great life. I have my ups and downs with my parents, but that won't stop me from loving them during rough times. They were there during the most difficult times of my life - always by my side. That is what real love truly is. Always forgiving, ready to support me, making sure I'm getting the right education, making sure I'm healthy, and so much more.

My parents are my adoptive parents but they are my true parents. Confusing? Not really when you think about it. Real parents are different from biological parents. Biological parents give you life, however real parents are the ones who feed you, the ones who provide you with an education, love you, help you when you're upset, tuck you in at night, and care for you. My biological parents can and will always hold a special place forever in my heart but I really owe it to my adoptive parents. My true parents. When people struggle with their adoption issues I will be there to help them. I'll be there with a listening, open ear because I can relate. I'll treat them with kindness and everlasting patience.

Like my true parents. As a true friend.

Marisa Cox was born in Fernando De La Mora, Paraguay on March 11,1995. She is fourteen years old and enjoys singing and acting. She hopes that someday she will become either a Social Studies teacher or a Therapist.

BAR HARBOR CHRIS OR MY FIRST CASE OF GIRL LOVE

by Juli Jeong Martin

sun bleached hair short
and spiked white tips
standing tall
and narrow on the docks
in a navy blue l.l. bean fleece
you were the dyke of my dreams.

i serenaded you with Ani songs
when i knew that you weren't listening
we traded scar stories and
you let me take the photograph
that i would, at two week's end
collage into my summer's memories
surreptitiously
tucked between smiling friends.

when i drove the boat into the wake
of lobster buoy waves
you stood out on the mast and laughed
emerging soaked with salty spray
that bullshit grin spread wide across your face.

i imagined how your smile
would feel against mine.
that bullshit grin spread
warm across my skin.
i pretended that i would know what to do.

i was fifteen and femme
tucking tank tops into bras
exposed thighs and long hair
flirting with the pretty boys
but always waiting for you.

you were my first
case of girl love
unrequited but
felt deep in every pore
my body called out to you
like the Ani songs i sang
quietly to myself.

standing tall and narrow on the docks
abstract desire became tangible lust
brimming with the certainty
that straight girls didn't feel this way
that wanting you was altogether
everything i'd always thought of
skinned shins and
hair short spiked white tips.

a boat and the backdrop
of Mount Desert skyline
in an l.l. bean fleece
you were the dyke of my dreams.

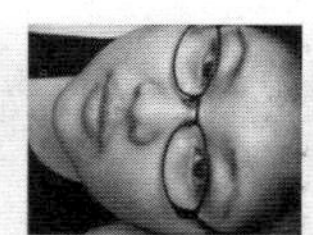

Find more of Juli's thoughts on pages 47, 72, 122, and 142.

Onni and Me: A Lifelong Search for an Asian Role Model

by Hanna Sofia Jung Johansson

Even though I always have felt a strong connection to my Swedish adoptive family (my mum, dad, and older brother), at the same time I also have felt a strong feeling of alienation. Perhaps my longing for an older sister arose from my feeling of being different? Maybe it was not about wishing for a role model with a similar appearance, but only a wish for an 'ordinary' older sister? Many of my friends had older sisters whom they could ask things that teenagers might not want to ask their mum about. It can be difficult for young Asian female adoptees to get advice from their Western mums as they have not experienced prejudices about Asian women. In hindsight, I wonder if my longing for an older sister was an unconscious wish for an Asian role model.

The question "How should I put make up on my slanted eyes?" can be one of the most common questions among East Asian female adoptees. That is a question most Westerners do not have an answer for... At times, I wonder if I would've worn more make up or been more interested in fancy clothing as a teenager if I had had an Asian role model in my life back then. Instead, I was forced to either explore how to use make up and to find clothes that fit an East Asian body on my own or to care about other things as my mum's advice did not fit an Asian daughter. The sleeves and legs on the trousers were still too long for me no matter how much she tried to help! I chose instead to spend hours in the stable and to read tons of books instead of caring about fashion. When I started to be interested in East Asian fashion in my mid-20s, I looked at some books and visited some stores, but I seldom tried any of the clothes on. I simply did not know how to put them on and I was too embarrassed to ask the ladies in the stores.

As an adult I finally got a sort of older sister in my godparent LenaKim, whom I met in the Adopterade Koreaners Förening (AKF), the first adoptee association founded by adoptees in the world. In the beginning, I sometimes felt a bit shy in front of her. Perhaps this is because she is older and has so much more experience with adoption issues and of our birth country South Korea than I do? The foundation of our relationship was probably laid at the moment as I asked her if she could buy me chopsticks and spoons during one of her homeland visits. She said 'yes' and

> Onni is one of the Korean words for 'older sister'.
> It is common among Koreans to use words for being relatives
> even for people with whom they are not related to.

promised to deliver the utensils at AKF's summer camp in the archipelago outside Stockholm.

As we got to know each other better, LenaKim became that Asian female role model I had been searching for my whole life. At first, it felt a bit awkward to be cared about by a woman I hardly knew and who also happened to be Korean just like me. LenaKim probably felt my hesitation and chose to let me take the next step in our relation.

Shortly after the camp, LenaKim became my godmother. In the beginning, this mainly meant that we talked on the phone, exchanged emails and met when I had business in Stockholm. As our contact and my visits at AKF events became more frequent, our relationship started to resemble some kind of sisterhood. LenaKim took me to all kinds of Asian food stores, furniture stores,

Korean restaurants, made lunch and told me about her travels to South Korea.

When I am out walking on my own or visiting different places, I feel worried about people's looks, questions and comments. When I'm with my godmother I feel more secure. I trust that she, or we together, can handle such things. I simply feel less alone when I meet ignorant and nosy people.

We also discussed and exchanged many thoughts, feelings and experiences about being an Asian adopted woman in Sweden. The more we talked, the more it felt like I finally had met someone who reflected myself, partly physically as LenaKim is Korean too, but also emotionally and intellectually. With LenaKim's support it became easier for me to dig deeper into my feelings and thoughts about adoption, South Korea, and about being both Swedish and Asian, yet not 100% either. I can discuss my deepest thoughts about these subjects with LenaKim as she respects me and listens, although we are very different in many other ways. She seldom says what is right or wrong, but instead she gives her own response, pieces of advice or shares her own experiences. No questions are too banal, weird or forbidden. I can also ask her for pieces of advice about fashion, clothes, and make up even though I am still not excessively interested in such things.

"Maybe this is how it feels to have an older sister?", I think at times and I often call her Onni. I also wonder if my life had been different if I have had an Asian or adopted role model as a child. Onni is in many ways a role model for me today, but that does not compensate for the lack of such a role model as a child nor the loss of my birth mum. I think that Onni is right, it is good with siblings and friends with a similar background - but that is NOT the same as a role model, an older person.

However, Onni's and my relationship is not easy as every time I meet her, I am reminded of how little I know about Korea, my birth culture, and my roots. Unconsciously our relation touches upon the loss of the first Korean woman in my life: Omma, my birthmother. The unconscious memory of this primal loss complicates my relation to Onni. This insecurity has sometimes led me to test our relationship. But still, Onni has continued to be there for me. I have always been afraid of hurting Onni with the many complex feelings that I expose in our relation as it hosts both feelings of security, happiness, loss, and pain. Over time, I have become more certain that many of the feelings are not connected to our relationship, but instead to my separation from my biological mother.

As a child, and even as an adult, I could feel completely alone, as though people who claim to care about me are living in some kind of parallel world and never fully understand my feelings of being different. It is like our roads never really meet no matter how much we try. However, my relation with Onni and with other international adoptees, though, somehow makes me feel less alone and less alien.

Hanna Sofia Jung Johansson was adopted from South Korea to Sweden at an age of 4 months in 1976. Hanna Sofia's text is about the importance of ethical role models for transracial adoptees. Hanna Sofia holds a PhD in Science and Technology Studies and is a board member of Korean @doptees Worldwide.

where do i fit

my difference

by Alysia Sutupa Larson

Sometimes in life you realize that you're different. Sometimes it's a big difference, like knowing that you were meant to be President of the United States, but usually it's a difference that is only whispered throughout your life. You realize it every day and sometimes you wish that you could just scream it out at the top of your lungs that "Yes, I am different!" People who are not faced with this problem may never understand your dilemma and some may even tell you to just stop being dramatic about it, but an adopted teen feels all the normal pressures of being a teenager and more.

I was adopted when I was sixteen months old from Calcutta, India. My parents have always been gracious and loving. I was raised in a small town in Minnesota. I went to a Christian school and life was great. Then this feeling of uncertainty grew. I knew something was off but I couldn't place exactly what. I then realized it was me. I was the thing that was off. Me, with my dark chocolate skin, my midnight black hair, and don't forget the warm brown eyes. In all of my class pictures, I am the only one with the physical characteristics that offset everybody else. I am dark to their light. My friends were the best friends anybody could have, but still I was different.

The fact that I was different kept replaying over and over again in my teenage girl mind. Society wreaked havoc on my self esteem. I wasn't the tall, slim blonde with the fair porcelain skin and bright blue eyes. I was the total opposite. All of my friends said that they wished that they could have my dark skin and although that helped a little bit, it still made me realize I was different. These feelings only got stronger as I got older. Everyone told me I was a beauty, but I still hated seeing pictures of me with my "white" friends and family. I always saw the difference. I have a younger adopted brother that is from Calcutta, India as well, and it helped when he got added to the family pictures. At least someone looked like me, I thought. It didn't help when my friends would get frustrated that in the pictures with me they looked so much paler. I felt horrible for being in pictures but strangely elated because I knew they wanted to be darker. They even went to tanning beds to get darker! I felt like maybe I was a little bit more beautiful because they wanted to be like me, well at least have my dark skin. As I got older the feelings got stronger that I was different but suddenly I realized that's what made me unique. Society and Hollywood suddenly made the "Diversity" move and there were more people of color coming up all over: in magazines, in movies, on television. I wasn't the only one anymore. I was astonished to see all these colored men and women and more surprised to find that they were indeed beautiful. I found that I was like these gorgeous women. They had smooth chocolate skin and thick black hair. They even had brown eyes! I still struggle with being different and I know that most of my friends won't understand what I mean unless they were suddenly the only "white" people in a group.

I went back to India when I was twelve and the sudden realization that this was my homeland made me want to cry with relief. Everyone here had the same physical characteristics as me. I saw many beautiful people and knowing that I was from the same place did great wonders for my heart and self esteem. I went back to the United States wishing that I wouldn't have to feel out of place anymore, but I still did. I knew that practically nobody was judging me but I still felt out of place. I once wrote a blog and for every "A" in the blog I highlighted it in brown. The "a" was for my name and the brown was for me. At the end of the blog I wrote, "Do you see all the brown marks? They look weird and out of place don't they?" Well welcome to my life. I feel so out of place."

I still feel out of place but I know that I need to accept that my differences are what makes me unique. I know that people have told that to me many times but I never took it to heart. Even when I realize that I am beautiful inside and out, I still slip and fall back into my mindset that I am different and that it's a bad thing.

Don't be upset if you keep falling back into the mindset just keep working at accepting that you are beautiful and unique. It's something you have to find out for yourself. Don't worry about trying to fit in or trying to feel a certain way. If you need to cry and feel out of place, let yourself. I know that once I finally came to terms with being different life was so much easier. I stopped pretending that I could fit in. I realized that I was made to stand out. Embrace the difference and become what you were supposed to be and do what you were supposed to do. You've been given a chance by being adopted. Make something of that chance. Don't spoil it. There are many others that wish they had the same chance as you do. Let the difference make you better. And know that there was a lonely, out of place, different girl out there that felt the same way and still does at times. God bless you all, and I hope you find out that your difference is what makes you a treasure.

Alysia Larson is a 19 year old adoptee from Isanti, MN. She goes to college at North Dakota State University and hopes to return to her birth town of Calcutta, India again someday. Her article "My Difference" helped her realize that being unique is something that is to be cherished.

Sock Bunnies

by Jessica Emmett

For many years I have talked and been told about my adoption. Before the time of Lifebooks, I had no item from my birthmother, but I did have a set of photographs taken of me by my foster family and a single hand-made sock bunny. Until I was a late teen I had not even thought much about my foster family. I know as little about them as my birthmother. Sadly they were not in any of the photos they took but I was fascinated by the sock bunny, my first toy that I carried everywhere even after my adoption at the age of one.

I felt that I might have a chance to understand my foster family if I somehow reproduced the loving sock bunny. I was lucky enough to have a short art residency at the Chinese Arts Centre in the UK in 2006. The first half of the residency I asked people to send me second hand or unwanted socks they had. I made 20 bunnies myself... painstakingly. In the second half of the residence I set up a website with all the details of each sock bunny and any details I had of them. I then invited people into the gallery to adopt one. It wasn't simply a case that just anyone could adopt one, but that there was paper work, commitment, responsibility. Since there were only 20, I turned down quite a few people as I acted as a social worker. Once someone had adopted a sock bunny, they were asked to give progress reports in the form of blogs on the website.

It has often bothered me that when I tell I'm adopted, I am told how wonderful adoption is. I did this project to see if I could teach people the extent of the procedures that are involved with adoption. The original project was done in 2006. I have made a few since, and have mainly given the sock bunnies to all kinds of adopted people. This idea still seems to have life, and I hope to continue with new sock bunny projects.

If you'd like to see the website of the original project you can go to **www.sockbunnies.com** Post photos of your sock bunny on the Pieces of Me: Who do I want to be? Facebook page.

And if you would like to bring your own sock bunny to life, please turn the page for how to!

Jessica Emmett is a 27-year old artist from the UK. Her "Sock Bunnies" & "Tag Cloud" art (see page 136) looks at her foster family and identity as an adoptee with a complex history. Jessica continues to work with adoption as a subject for her art and workshops.

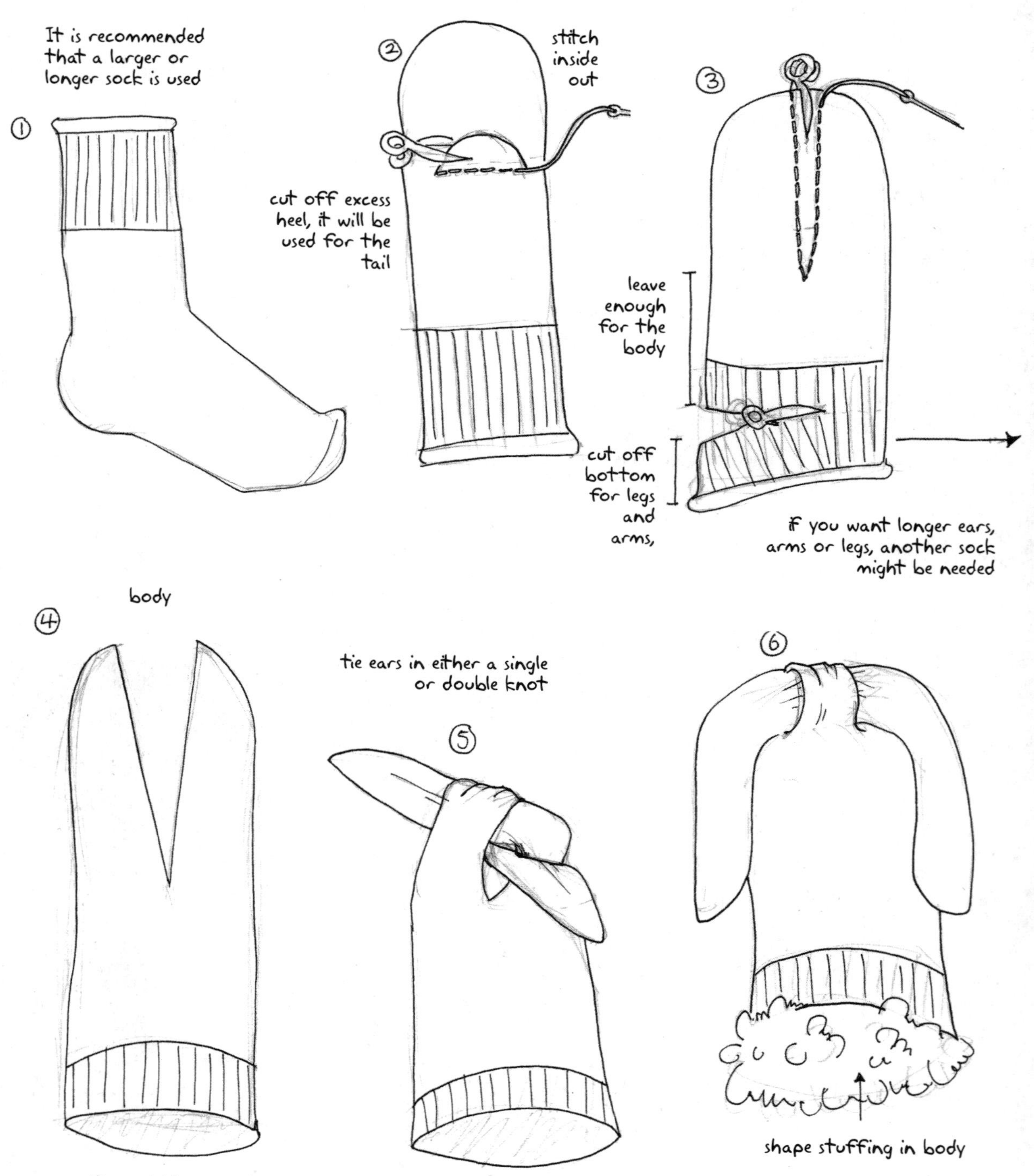
It is recommended that a larger or longer sock is used
①
②
stitch inside out
cut off excess heel, it will be used for the tail
③
leave enough for the body
cut off bottom for legs and arms,
if you want longer ears, arms or legs, another sock might be needed
body
④
turn right way out
tie ears in either a single or double knot
⑤
⑥
shape stuffing in body

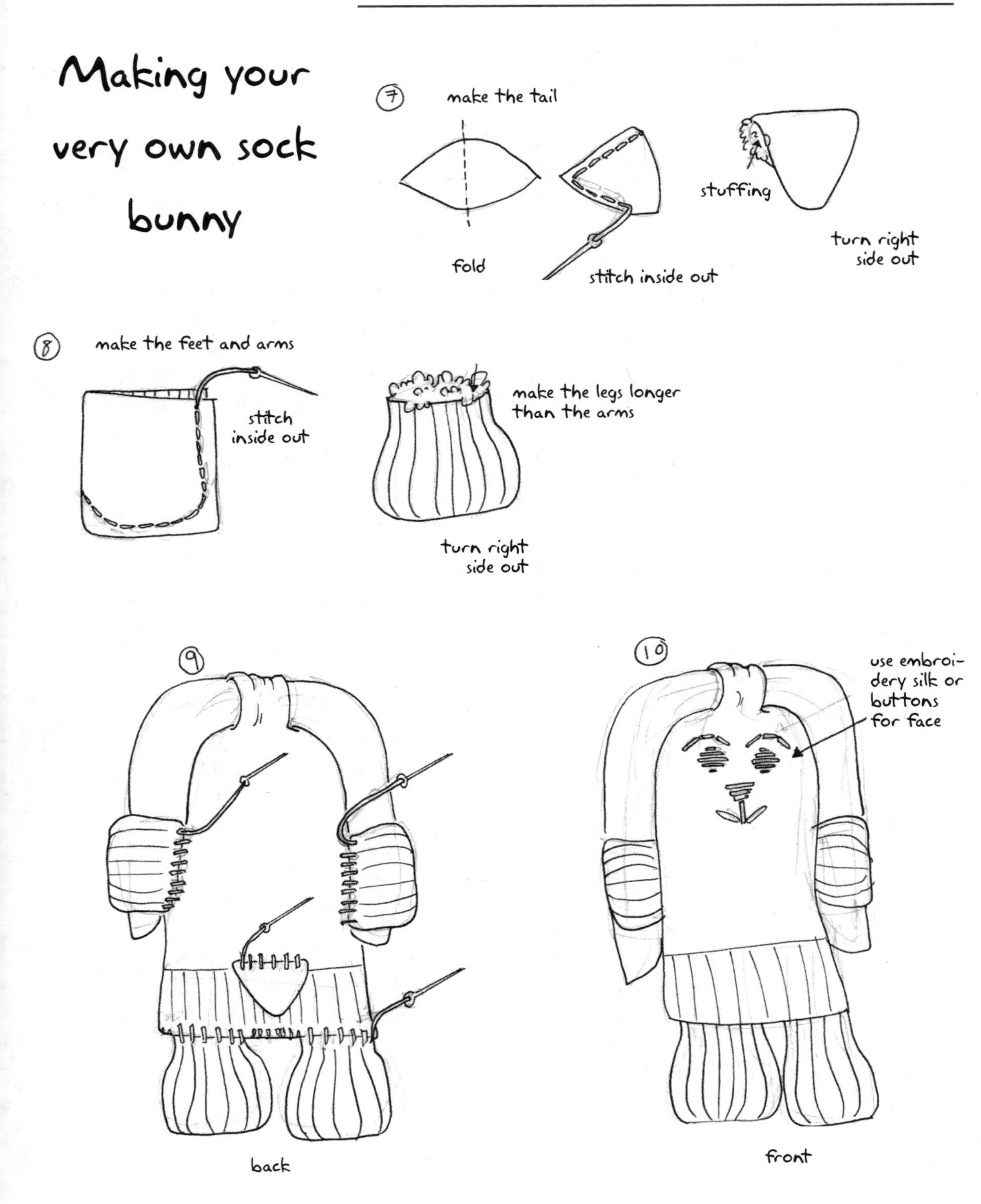
Making your very own sock bunny
7 make the tail
fold
stitch inside out
stuffing
turn right side out
8 make the feet and arms
stitch inside out
make the legs longer than the arms
turn right side out
9
back
10
use embroi-dery silk or buttons for face
front

blood matters

By Angie Johnston

Blood is the life force in our bodies. It is not my soul or my spirit, but it is the part of me that carries life to the rest of my body. It is the foundation of my physical existence. In every culture, blood symbolizes vitality and life. In our stories (books, movies, myths), blood can speak to many things; where we come from, purification, sacrifice and death. If someone sheds their blood for another it is the most sacrificial gift they can offer to them. The blood we carry is proof of our existence, our connection to our lineage and the rest of humankind. It says in bright red letters **i am here** and **i matter**. I wish that I had known the value of whose blood I carried sooner. The truth that my blood carries parts of my being that can never be erased, parts that matter to who I am.

I grew up adopted, with the privilege of having a family who took me in as their own. They loved me as if they had given birth to me. In fact, I felt special because I was adopted. I had been chosen. I wore my position of being chosen as a badge of honor, wanting and needing to believe that the connection I had with my adopted family carried more weight than my bloodline. My biological parents were drug addicts as far as I knew, and my mother was mentally ill. Through the process of events, my birthparents were not able to care for me. I did not want those details to matter in who I thought myself to be.

As I grew up, especially in high school and college, I remember having many debates and discussions about adoption. It didn't matter if I was in a class, a small group or just watching a movie with a friend. If the subject of blood in relation to birth, love, or family came up I was the first one to stand up and say, "Your blood doesn't matter." I thought it was not that important who gave you life or who gave that person life. The only thing that matters is who has impacted your life since you've been alive. I didn't realize both could be true.

I recently read a yearbook from high school and it confirmed how I thought my friends saw me. They perceived me as someone grounded and solid, someone who knew where she was headed. If they could have looked past my strong opinions and tough persona they would have seen someone who was vulnerable, scared, and witnessed my "hauntings."

My "hauntings" were experiences of randomness, which would often and unexpectedly fill me. I was anything but solid. It seemed there were as many people in the world as there are grains of sand on the beach. In the midst of the billions, what did I matter? Unconsciously what flowed through my veins were the "questions": Why was I here in the first place? Where did I come from? Who did I come from? Is my existence on this planet good? The feelings that came from these unanswered questions left me insecure and filled with doubt. I was making life decisions out of this mind-set.

As people (whether we are adopted or not), we all need to know, in our minds and in the core of our heart, that our existence here is good. We need to know that it is a good thing that we were born. In order to have this truth we need to make room for our "beginning": the good, hard, and

as people (whether we are adopted or not), we all need to know, in our minds and in the core of our heart, that our existence here is good.

even ugly parts of our start in life. It wasn't until I acknowledged my story: my blood mother and father, who they were, and the truth of where I come from that I had room in my heart to see my own value. It didn't matter what their problems or their failures were. It just mattered that their life and their parent's life... meant something. Their existence mattered. Of course, my birthparents are not the full weight of my significance, but without them, their stories, their parents, their blood, I would not exist, and certain characteristics about who I am would not be.

I was 28 years old and seven months pregnant with my first child when I traveled with my biological sister (who I had reconnected with 5 years earlier) to meet our birthmother. She lives in a half way home for people with mental illness. Truth be told, she is mostly disconnected from reality. Nonetheless, seeing her, touching her, hearing her story, even how she gave birth to me, I believe set the stage for me to give birth to my first daughter with a different understanding of who we all were. It was soon after her birth, one day while nursing her, that I really understood the bond between her and I, and I felt the importance of blood coursing through my flesh. I could see in her face and feel in my heart what I was to her. No other person on the planet could be what I was to her. I knew that if I were to never see her again she would always carry me, through her blood, for the rest of her life. I wept. For the first time in my life I was thankful for my birthmother. I said it aloud, and felt space in my heart to give and receive love like I never had before.

If you are adopted, then it is true that the connection you had with your birthparents was broken. To make sense of this, especially in our emotions, it is easy to negate their importance, or for others, to overemphasize the importance of their birthparents. Either way we diminish our own worth and shrink our hearts to live and be loved.

I needed to have a blood transfusion so to speak. My adopted parents gave me many wonderful things (that's a whole other story), but they didn't give me birth. I needed to have my story and my mother and father running through my veins again. I needed their blood to give me oxygen. My breaths are much deeper and fuller now. Whoever they are and wherever they are, I am full of thanks to them. Thank you James and Susan for giving me life, for giving me blood. Because of you I exist and that is good.

Angie Johnston is an adult adoptee, married and loves being a mother to her three children. She has been a counselor in private practice for the last 15 years. Angie would love to see all adopted children grow up embracing their own vital, important, and unique stories.

Copy this page (especially if you have borrowed this book from the library!)
Draw how you feel right now, today, in this moment. You can do this again and again. It's a great way to express how you feel in times of joy or struggle or even in response to something in this book.

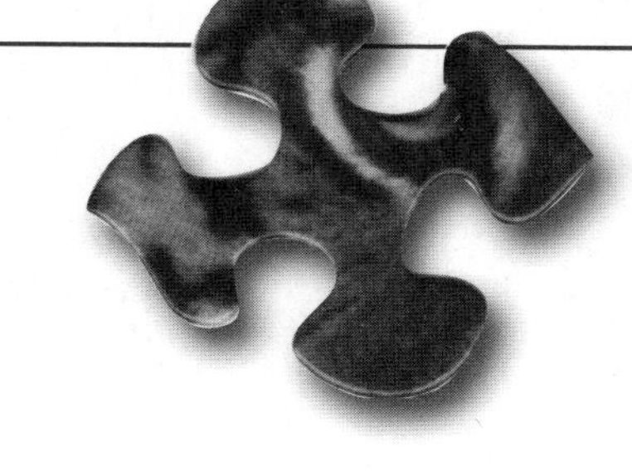

Stolen Pieces

Let's face it, being adopted has challenges.

Someone once said that adoption comes out of loss. I think that's insightful. All of us who are adopted have lost something – our "first" family, our birth culture, our connection to flesh and blood, our roots, our stories.

That is what this section is about – those things we've lost. In here you will find stories, songs, poems, and expressions about losing the birthmother, father, or child; losing connection to a culture or country; losing our innocence or our childhood; struggling each day; losing our roots; and losing our way.

They are things taken from us without our choice or consent. We didn't choose to be adopted. But we live with what we've lost, with what's been taken from us.

These are our Stolen Pieces, those things we can never get back but what we need in order to complete our puzzle. Those things taken from us that we are trying to figure out how to fill the void.

These are the pieces that never made it into the box, but we wish would have...

They say...

by Paula Louise O'Loughlin

They say I was just a baby, what possibly could I know?

They say I was just a baby, what possibly could I feel?

They say I was just a baby, what possibly could I remember?

They say I was just a baby, how much would I really lose?

They say I was just a baby, and that I wouldn't really notice.

They say I was just a baby, and that I wouldn't really care.

They say I was just a baby, and that it wouldn't really matter.

They say I was just a baby, and that she could be replaced.

They say I was just a baby, and that I wouldn't crave her touch.

They say I was just a baby, and that I wouldn't miss her love.

They say I was just a baby, and that time will heal all wounds.

They say I was just a baby, and that I'd never know any different.

They say I was just a baby, and that life would go on as planned.

They say I was just a baby, and that the pain could be loved away.

They say I was just a baby, and that I'd never feel as if I'd ever lost her.

Paula O'Loughlin, a Korean adoptee, is a teacher, mother of two, and an avid connoisseur of dolsot bibimbap and yukgaejang. Traveling to Korea with her husband to adopt their son had a profound effect on Paula and her identity as an adoptee. Her poem "They Say" talks about the impact that her Korean mother has had on her life.

How I Felt About My Baby

by Hannah Chadwick-Dias

For school, I had to do an interesting project for my health class, which was taking care of a robotic baby. The robotic babies are like real babies except they aren't alive. They do just about everything real babies do, and they brought me a lot of joy. I got to keep the baby for three days and was very sad to give it away. On the third day, during lunch recess, when my teacher was collecting them, I felt too sad to return it, so I gave it to one of my friends. After my friend had returned the baby, I had feelings I couldn't explain.

When I got home, I still cried, felt sad, and was tired because I had to wake up in the night to feed and change the baby the night before. So I took a long nap thinking that I would feel better afterward. When I woke up, I still had this feeling like I wanted to cry. I went to my grandma's house and explained what I was going through. She helped me feel a little better, but the next day I still felt like I was going to cry if I talked to anyone. I felt like I couldn't talk to anyone on the phone and especially face-to-face.

That night during dinner, I brought up the baby thing to my dad and instantly I burst into tears. When my mother said that maybe giving up the baby was difficult for me because my birthparents left me when I was a little baby. Finally I figured out how I was feeling but couldn't tell my family because I was still not up to telling anyone. You see, I was adopted when I was 12 years old and had to leave everything behind back in China. Then I cried and cried until I had no more tears left and went to bed.

The morning when I woke up, I cried some more. In the afternoon I felt that I was ready to tell my family about how I was feeling. My mother understood right away and I was grateful for that. I told my family that I was feeling sad because I had never known my birthparents and probably never would. That I was feeling sad because I was trying to picture my mother giving me away because she couldn't take care of me or she wanted a boy.

Hannah Chadwick-Dias is 17 and lives with her family in Humboldt County, California. She was adopted from China when she was 12 and a half. Hannah overcame many daily challenges, the biggest was adjusting to school since she did not attend school in China due to visual impairment. Most public schools in China don't allow students with disabilities. Hannah is now attending high school and hopes to go on to university.

I cry
but no one comes
This room
with many beds
with many children
with much noise
with no mothers

I wonder
alone at night
surrounded by family
so much gratitude
so much love
why there is so much
and yet, so little

I rage
in someoné arms
I rage
with every drink I take
with every blunt I smoke
the rage is unanswerable
the mother not found

I search
with desperation
with despair
with hope
the sounds of mothers
calling for the children
cries from keyboards
To come home
not mine
never mine

And so,
I cry
for that room
with so many beds
with so many children
with no mothers
for myself

for more of Eun Mi's poetry see pages 51, 60, 73, 121, and 148.

Looking for Mary

Mary had a baby
But motherhood couldn't coexist
With the life she had to lead.

Something was broken
And one half will continually search for the other
Forever to remain
Open.

What happened to her baby?
She was loved in safety
A heart cared for and protected
But out of tune with its surroundings.

An open heart always searching
It can feel the pulse
Of life beating through it.

Two open hearts,
Both always searching,
Slowly, gradually, beating in time.

'Grace'
22 March 2006

'Grace' is a twenty-six year old adoptee from London, England. She is currently studying medicine and has recently been able to contact some friends of her birthmother who should would like to meet someday. See her article "Understanding my Birthparents" on page 16.

I can't be loved

By Judy M. Miller

Her mind churns with the "what's" and "why's." What if she was with her birthmother? What would life be like in her birth country? Why doesn't she live with her birth family? Sometimes, my daughter feels she is not where she should be.

She came into the room on the hip of the orphanage nanny, her sweet smiling face covered in bug bites. The recently shaven hair was growing out; it promised to be thick. Dreamy eyes searched the room and found mine. She put her thumb in her mouth and kept looking at me, no one else. I couldn't smell her, but I knew that the stained and mismatched clothes she wore stunk. My heart threatened to drown in the waves of love that surged through it.

They called her name and I rushed to take my beautiful daughter. She came to me easily, as if she had always done so. So close to me, she felt enmeshed within my body. She reeked – of dirtiness and something unhealthy. She felt full of sadness and resignation, as if she was searching for something and I was not quite it.

I had waited so long to hold my daughter. All of forever slipped away as she snuggled closer. Emotional distress emanated from her. If I could have opened up my skin and put her inside of me, I would have - safe, warm, and deeply loved. I prayed that the love I had for her would help her through it. I prayed for a bottomless well of patience. Shattering screams erupted from somewhere deep within her. Her crying was overwhelming, profound anguish. You would have to be inhuman not to feel it.

I would literally drop everything at the first sound of the ear-splitting shriek of her cry. Gathering her up, I would pull her in as close to me as I could, and rock her, often crying with her. As she grew older, she began to talk about what she was feeling. "I don't want to be here!", "You're not my "real" mother; you're a babysitter!", "Why did she give me up?", and "She didn't love me!" My daughter was tormented by pain, anger and grief. It was difficult to hear. I had no answers for her; I had not been given any details about her birth family or their adoption plan for her. I just kept telling her that I loved her, and she would fight that, screaming, "No you don't." My daughter felt she wasn't worthy of anyone's love because someone hadn't loved her enough to keep her. I would continue to hold her until she was spent and she would succumb to sleeping in my arms, only to awaken as though nothing had happened – as delightful and sweet as ever.

The years have sped by. My daughter has grown into a bright funny and insanely curious person. She is on the cusp of becoming a woman. But, every year, around her birthday, it unravels. It's as if some internal clock ticks away and then the alarm goes off as loudly as a thunder clap – and it all starts again.

What starts again? The deep-rooted primal pain – and I experience it as it revisits my daughter. With each year it has grown, garnering power over her, not allowing closure.

"Are you afraid I won't love you?"

She nodded her head and began to cry.

Judy M. Miller is a mom to four busy, busy multiracial, multi-cultural kids (home grown and adopted), ranging from the ages of 7-16. Her articles and stories have appeared in parenting magazines and her essay, "Souls Speak", is featured in *A Cup of Comfort for Adoptive Families*. She is a contributing writer for Grown in My Heart: An Adoption Network, writes at the International Mom Blog, and mentors and teaches classes to prospective adoptive parents and adoptive parents.

Dear Mum
by Chris Abbott

When the cord was cut
You gave me away
I waited for you
Every day of each week
Nose stuck to the window
With the squeak of the gate
Staring at faces
That passed in the street
Needed you
But you never came back.

Chris Abbott is fifty eight years old, an adoptee from London. At the moment she carries a stitched up bag. It holds loads of bits pieces and jumbled messages. Many have their roots from her teenage years.

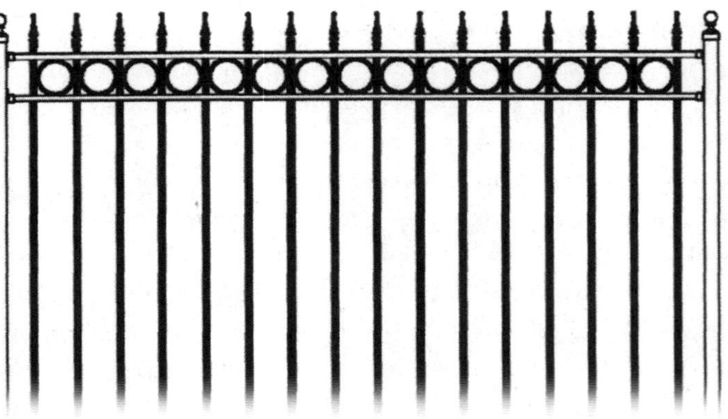

The Burn on my Hand

by Júli Jeong Martin

There's a story my mom tells about when I was a little girl, maybe five or six. I was standing on a chair next to the ironing board, helping her de-lint a sweater. She warned me not to touch the iron because it was hot, but I did anyway, and burned the back of my hand. I didn't say anything, didn't let on that I had hurt myself, just continued to studiously remove pills from the sweater's surface with packing tape. She later found me in the bathroom trying to treat the wound myself.

My parents told me I was adopted at a very young age, as I one day announced that I knew why I didn't look like my brother and sister – "because I didn't come from mommy's tummy." I vividly remember being about four years old and sitting on the couch, staring off out the window, dreaming of my mythic homeland where all the hair was thick and black like mine. People were always telling me how beautiful my hair was – no matter their intentions, it only served to single me out as foreign.

At five I was just entering kindergarten, in a class where I was one of two people of color and in a school where I was one of three. At five I announced with glee to my mother, "Look Mom! Another Juliana!" upon spotting another Asian girl. At five I already knew what it meant to be different.

Which brings us back to the bathroom and the burn I wouldn't have had if only I'd listened to my mother. The burn that would sell me out as a bad child, an unworthy child, a child who didn't belong. The burn that could return me to the backwards little country that didn't want me in the first place; the burn that would render me an orphan twice. I could see red letters on official looking papers: **TOUCHED THE IRON AFTER BEING TOLD NOT TO**.

I don't know where this anxiety came from, I can't recall who first planted the seed of fear in my mind. Perhaps it was kids in my school who taunted me, who said that because my parents bought me they could send me back. Or maybe it was the underlying feeling of being the odd one out, of not belonging. Maybe it was my browner skin, my slanted eyes, my beautiful hair, and the ways in which these things separated me from my family and everyone I knew.

> I don't know where the anxiety comes from. I can't recall who first planted the seed of fear in my mind.

She tells this story to me because it frightened her to realize that she had a child who would internalize and hide her pain. She tells this story because she thinks it will help explain who I became a decade later, still someone who internalizes and hides her pain, still someone who curls up in the bathroom to treat wounds I wouldn't have if I just listened to my mother.

My family would attribute this early incident and later behaviors to the mental illness that still keeps a tight hold on me. But to what do we attribute this illness? Is it biology? Imbalances of chemicals and faulty genes? Or is it something less organic?

People don't want to realize that there is trauma in being adopted, no matter how young you are when it happens. And there's a trauma in growing up adopted, too. There's a trauma in every person who asks you where your parents are when they're standing right beside you; there's a trauma in

> The editor's pen was well intentioned, but in its artful movements, it erased the foundation on which I build my life.

every teasing, every teacher that makes you tell the class why you were given up. There's a trauma in knowing that your parents will never understand how this feels, no matter how many times they say they do.

My story begins in a place that is frequently referred to as "a backwards" nation, "third world" country or perhaps just a "patriarchal" society. I call it the homeland.

At this point in my story, the faces are blurry, the characters undeveloped, their motivations unclear. At this point in my story, I had a different name: Hye Won. I don't know where it came from, whether it was the final parental act of a young, unwed mother or the careful construction of a seasoned social worker. All I know is that it is written in steady type on the handful of papers that are supposed to tell me who I am.

That's the thing, you see, my entire history is subject to change, open to revision. It's fiction, "based on a true story" and "inspired by actual events." There are always facts redacted, dates changed, something modified to make my story more beautiful. The editor's pen was well intentioned, but in its artful movements, it erased the foundation on which I build my life.

It has taken a lot to get me here. But where am I?

Sometimes I wonder if I am exceptional in my disability, or if this is just our story. Certainly I know other adoptees that are "better adjusted", but I wonder if this struggle is universal. The struggle to feel good enough, worthy, deserving. The struggle to not break down when people leave your life; to not see their absence as a mother leaving, never to return.

It isn't just abandonment, it's everything that follows, too. It's every glare, every stare, every question about where you came from, why you were abandoned, do you want to find your birthmother? It's every time you're asked if your father is your husband, because, well, that's just what Asian women do. Every playground rhyme that mocks your eyes, every child who says that you can't do that because you have black hair and every person who tries to guess "what" you are.

It's growing up in the midst of all this hatred, all the while being told by doctors, social workers, and adoptive parents that you don't feel any different. Having everyone you meet tell you how lucky you are to be chosen that way, and don't you feel grateful? It's always finding flaws in yourself and not the other, not the system. It's never knowing the word "racism" applied to you, because Asians are the model minority and hey, we're colorblind anyway. It's finding self-worth when there are no faces like yours, no one you can see living your pain and rising above, beyond.

My mother always called it "ignorance", and said that in my silence, I was superior. Today I stretch my vocal chords past her, past them, past history. Today I write my story: for the first time, not the last time, but for all time.

Juli Martin (AKA juli jeong martin) was adopted in December 1985 at the age of six months. She is a full time student at Oberlin College in Oberlin, OH majoring in Comparative American Studies. At Oberlin, Juli supplements her academic work through anti-oppression activism, art and late night baking. She recently printed her first chapbook which dealt with issues of transracial adoption, queerness, family and memory.
Find more of Juli's thoughts on pages 28, 72, 122, and 142.

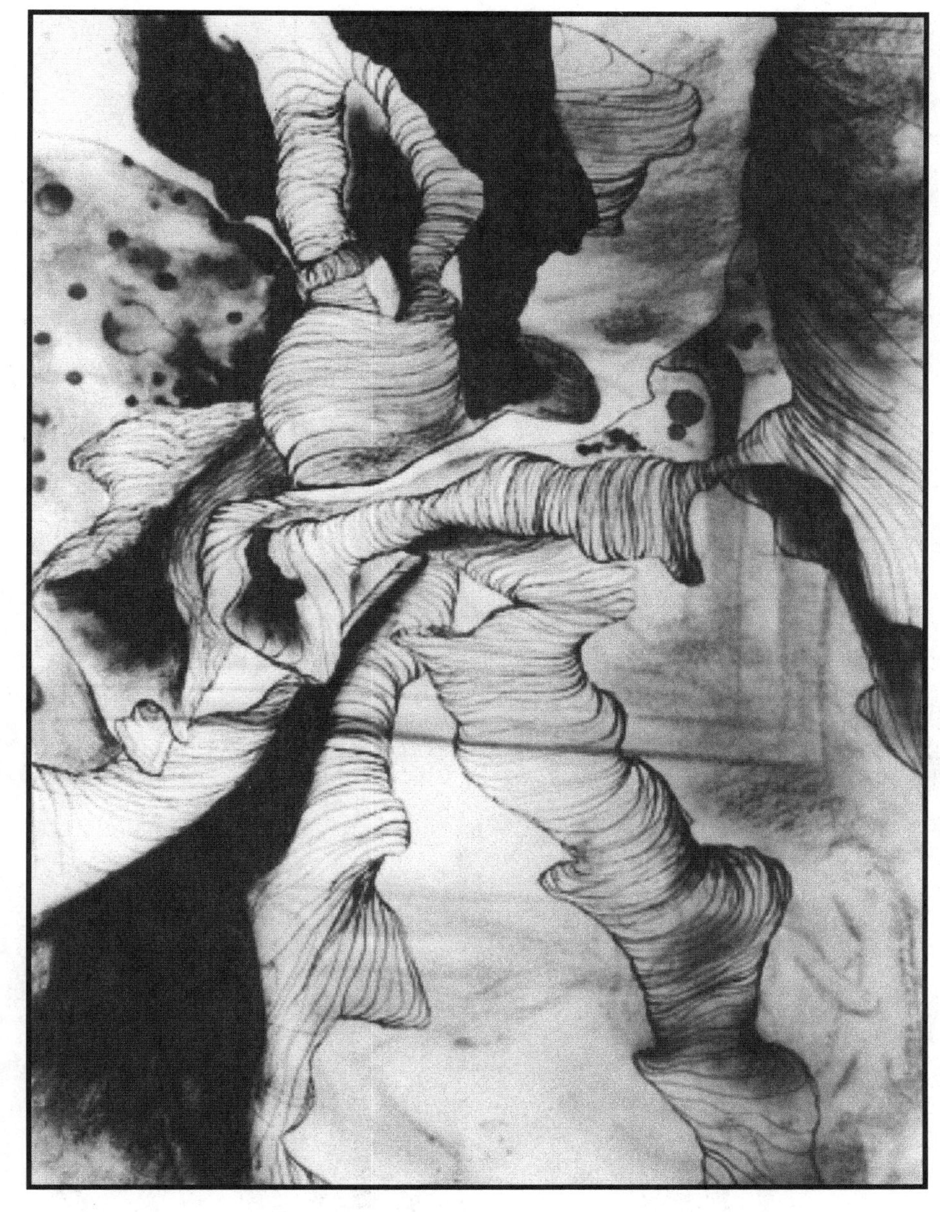

The Drain by Stacy K. Pearson

"The Drain" represents the exhausting nature of living as an adopted child in a family where you are the only person adopted. In my situation, my adoptive family consisted of my brother who is my adoptive parents' biological child, my adoptive parents, and me. We never spoke about adoption, never brought it up....always taboo. Each rope-like piece in this drawing represents a hidden emotion. All of the hidden emotions revolve or focus on one point, almost a vortex in life, which is adoption.
Find Stacy's other art on pages 9, 18, 52, 101, and 151.

My name is Amy Martin.

I was born in South Korea in May of 1975. I was adopted into an American family in November of 1975. My parents told me I was adopted when I was five. Up until then I didn't know I looked different.

Once I knew I was adopted, I told everyone. I told stories. Everyone knew.

I am an alien.

I was raised by wolves.

I hatched from a pod.

Once I knew, I began to feel different. And as I began to feel different, everyone knew.

I punched a girl in the face when she called me a "chink." Kids threw rocks at me as I walked down the street. I learned to alternate between cursing and creeping.

Still, I was and am very close to my parents. My family has always been supportive and loving. Yet I am just one of over 160,000 overseas korean adoptees...

...and each of our stories is different.

Some Thoughts about My Adoption

by Emma

I've struggled at times, even though I've been blessed with a loving adoptive family that has always been there for me throughout my twenty years of life. When I was born, my birthmother was unable to parent another child, and both men who might be my birthfather agreed to her adoption plan. My adoptive parents were with my birthmother in the delivery room when I was born, and the families have stayed in touch ever since. Adoption has never been a secret or a taboo topic in my family. Nonetheless, **I have always wondered about my birthparents, where I come from, who I am, how to fit in, and where I belong.**

My wish for acceptance and love stemmed from my feelings about adoption, although throughout my childhood if someone suggested that I would adamantly deny it. As a child, I did not understand how adoption affected me. While my adoptive family accepted and loved me wholeheartedly, I got into trouble at times because I would do anything my peers wanted me to do, just so I would be accepted by them.

As a young adult, I now understand that the genetic challenges I inherited from my biological family has a lot to do with why I've struggled at times and why my birthparents needed to make an adoption plan for me. But as a child, I didn't understand this. In elementary school I was a loner, preferring to live in the world of books. Sometimes I acted out, giving my family a very hard time. Today, in retrospect, I see that my misbehavior stemmed both from the challenges I was born with and from feeling dissatisfied, alone, and rejected no matter how hard my parents tried to help me feel loved and worthwhile.

My deeply rooted fear of rejection sometimes made it hard for me to make and sustain friends. As a kid, it was hard for me to understand why my birthparents gave me up. I felt like it wasn't even worth trying to make friends because they wouldn't like me and would leave me anyway. I clung to the friends I had to the point that sometimes I pushed them away. I was always so scared they would leave me. **Looking back I can see that I have always had a deep rooted fear of abandonment.**

Until the eighth grade I had successes in school, winning a big reading contest, my school's science fair, a local essay contest, making the honor roll, and learning martial arts. But by age 14 I'd lost track of how to achieve acceptance the right way. I hung out with the wrong crowd and didn't care. Things spiraled downhill, and I was headed for trouble. I didn't realize that the only reason these kids accepted me was that I would do just about anything to be part of their group. It didn't matter to me that these kids were using me. I just wanted to feel wanted. I lived for the feeling of being accepted; it got me high, and I would do nearly anything for that feeling. I was so lonely inside and so desperate to be needed and wanted that I took the road I never wanted to take. I wanted my birthparents to need and want me. It didn't matter to me that my adoptive parents loved and wanted me. Maybe I was unconsciously pushing them away in order to make my worst fear happen.

My parents, having tried everything to help me in my home community, sent me to a therapeutic wilderness program. That experience changed my life and the way I look at it. I spent nine weeks in the woods of Georgia reflecting on myself and my behaviors. Although this was the beginning of my awakening, it certainly wasn't the end of my challenges. After many struggles, programs and schools, when I finally graduated from high school I, like others, was both surprised and relieved.

The next fall I went to Dean College in Massachusetts and ended up doing incredibly well; I graduated from there with high honors and my associate's degree in criminal justice. Today, I am a college senior, thinking about graduate school. I have good friendships, a job and career plans, an apartment, and good relationships with my family.

Nonetheless, my life is still a constant battle. I struggle every day with my feelings. I realize these feelings are not going away. They are part of me and have been since the beginning. What has changed is how I cope with them. I no longer chase negative relationships just so I can feel wanted. I have learned that there are other ways to fill the void inside. I don't automatically get upset if someone rejects me or if I don't get invited to a party. I feel hurt inside, yes, but instead of jumping to the conclusion that I am fundamentally unlovable, I tell myself that the person had their reasons.

I have realized that I don't need to let my adoption issues and my biological challenges control my life. As I continue to face down my demons, I notice more and more adoption related issues within me. This awareness is important because I can help others understand my behaviors so that they don't retreat from me, perpetuating my rejection cycle. People sometimes see me as a piece of work; they don't understand why I react to things the way I do and that pushes them away. For the longest time I didn't know why I reacted the way I did either. I just accepted other people's view that I was crazy. But I have realized that I am not crazy at all. My unique life experiences have made me the way I am, and I like the person I am becoming. It is a huge step for me to be able to identify my behaviors, correct them, and explain them to friends and family.

One might think that being in an open adoption would lessen my feelings of rejection and abandonment, but open adoption has been a double edged sword for me. On the plus side, it's definitely better knowing who my birth family is, having access to them and to their health information as it changes over time.

But also, contact with my birthmother has made it abundantly clear to me why I'm better off with my adoptive family than with my birth family. If I hadn't known her and some of my birth siblings, I might always have wondered if I'd been better off living with my biological family. I know first hand that I've been better taken care of in my adoptive family.

On the other hand, the contact with my birthmother has been painful for me at times. The most painful thing has been that my birthmother hasn't always shown up when she said she would and doesn't always respond to me when I contact her by mail, e-mail, or Facebook. I hate reaching out to her and then waiting month after month for a reply. It makes me feel unwanted, unworthy, let down, and given away all over again. I want more control in the relationship with her; I resent that I'm supposed to respond to her when it suits her to get in touch again but she doesn't always treat me with the same regard. In a nutshell, while open adoption is definitely better for me than a closed one, the journey hasn't always been smooth.

I don't think that being adopted is something to be ashamed of or kept secret. I hope someday to live my life without adoption feelings pushing me around. I am working hard on developing coping skills and building a support system so I don't feel so alone. Instead of adoption issues running my life, I hope they become something that makes my life a little more interesting and meaningful.

Emma is a senior at Bridgewater State College and a criminal justice major. She hopes that her life experiences will help her find a career in the field of criminal justice that allows her to help others who are struggling. She still struggles with feelings about adoption from time to time but she doesn't allow these feelings to hold her back.

Glove and Ball by Stacy K. Pearson

This image was created specifically for my amazing biological father. He is an incredibly talented man with vision and strength. One of his biggest passions has been baseball. Ironically, growing up it was a passion of mine as well. A dream for us both has been to play a game of catch in the back yard.....for us there will be so, so much more than a simple leather glove and ball.
Find Stacy's other art on pages 9, 18, 49, 101, and 151.

Stacy K. Pearson and her biological father Don Mallory were reunited in 2008 after thirty-two long years. Stacy, of Grand Rapids, MI, has found inspiration for her artwork from the journey through adopted life, the incredible experience of reunion, and the undeniable love between father and daughter.

Thirteen Years

By Cami Olsen

Thirteen years of never knowing
Who they were, where they were going

Thirteen years of falling dreams
My heart was beginning to rip at the seams

Thirteen years of burning hope
I finally learned to accept, to cope

Thirteen years of yearning for
Something big, for something more

Thirteen years of grasping abstraction
Of a love so great, it was close to perfection

They left me because they loved me so
That the only thing they could do,

Was let go.

Cami Olson was born and raised to a young age in Dong Nai, Vietnam and was later adopted to an American mother. "Thirteen Years" is a reflection on how she struggled to understand why she was put up for adoption and who her parents really were.

We, with two mothers
Expect little
from the first
And everything
from the second
Promises were made
Contracts signed
Money delivered

The second strike
hits harder
Sometimes
The wound
from the first
never fully heals
Never scabs over
Enough
Always hits
the same spot

Eun Mi is a Korean adoptee in San Antonio, Texas. Her poems reflect the loss of mother, and the role it has played in her life. Eun Mi works as an Adult Protective Services investigator for the State of Texas. Eun Mi's other poetry can be found on pages 43, 60, 73, 121, and 148.

adopted and abused

by IAM

I was born in South East Asia during what Americans call the Vietnam War and adopted to a Caucasian family in Australia when I was approximately 6 months old. I don't know anything about my birth family as I have no official papers from my birth country.

I grew up in rural Australia with a number of other siblings born to my adoptive parents. I was often the only ethnic person in my community. I remember growing up and feeling different in my family and my community. No-one talked about my adoption except to say to me how "lucky" I was. I grew up feeling quite lonely despite being raised in a large and noisy family.

My adoptive parents rarely spoke of my birth family except to say they had been told my mother was probably a prostitute and my father likely was a soldier during the war. I grew up feeling a sense of shame about my mother and it wasn't until I was older and met the birthmother of another adoptee that I realized the likelihood of my mother being a prostitute was probably very far from the truth. What contributed most to my sense of shame while growing up as an adopted teenager was the sexual abuse I suffered at the hands of my immediate and extended adoptive family.

The abuse started as early as 8 years old and the last time it occurred, I was a young teenager. During the early years of abuse I remember telling my brother and sister (who were also very young) what my older cousin was doing to me, but they thought I was making it up and laughed. I never spoke up to anyone else and the abuse continued a number of times and he once included another older cousin. I felt dirty and ashamed but too afraid to speak up. During my early teens, I was abused by another cousin on the other side of the family and by my adoptive brother. Again, I never spoke up because I felt too ashamed. When the abuse occurred at the hands of my adoptive father, I didn't dare tell anyone because I didn't think people would believe me. His abuse was by far the most damaging to my sense of self and added to my inability to trust others. I felt ugly and horrible about myself and his constant bullying and singling me out from the other siblings made me feel like I didn't belong.

It wasn't until years later when I remembered all the things that had happened at the hands of these men that I realized I felt very angry inside. I felt bad about myself and believed that somehow, something about me must have given them a message that I could be touched and hurt and that it was okay. In my thinking, God is a man, so did that mean I could never trust him and that he didn't care about my needs either? I felt more alone now because I couldn't trust God and I couldn't trust my "family." I believed being the only adopted one made me different enough for them to think they could do this type of thing without feeling it was wrong. I had heard my adoptive father often say that blood was thicker than water.

I was 18 years old when I first broke down, crying hysterically because the movie that I'd been watching had suddenly made me remember those bad things that had happened to me too. It was like my whole life had suddenly opened up into a big black pit and my soul was lost somewhere down in its depths. I cried for months afterwards and my boyfriend had little understanding of why I was suddenly so depressed and feeling suicidal. I felt so ashamed to tell him what had happened to me. I felt somehow that it must have been my fault, that I was ugly and had somehow deserved the pain I felt. I struggled in my first sexual relationship with my boyfriend as I subconsciously connected sex with shame, and I felt angry at men.

I was 19 when I eventually told my adoptive mum what had happened. I'd been suicidal and struggling with no support. I told her because I was desperate for someone to talk to. I also told her she couldn't tell anyone else because I felt so ashamed and I was scared of my father finding out that I'd told his "forbidden secret". My adoptive mum believed me and confirmed later that what I'd said was true. It wasn't until a few years later that I realized how much she struggled to deal with the secret I'd told her. She had become suicidal and probably contemplated walking away from her marriage. When this happened I felt a double dose of guilt. I blamed myself for exposing the abuse and causing my adoptive mother serious grief and pain because she never sought help for herself to deal with the situation.

A few years after telling my adoptive mother, I eventually asked my adoptive sister whether it had ever happened to her and she confirmed no. In my mind this proved the abuse had happened to me because I wasn't biologically connected to the abusers.

At the recommendation of one of my boyfriends, during my early twenties I finally sought professional help to deal with the sexual abuse and how it was impacting my life. The counselling I received while cutting off contact from my adoptive family for a few years finally helped me to heal. I was able to put the sexual abuse in perspective and I had to challenge and relearn my thoughts and behaviors. The ways in which sexual abuse had impacted my life were numerous and it wasn't until I dealt with these issues that I was finally able to see that I also had adoption issues. Hence, during my later twenties I spent a few years understanding my adoption and how it had impacted my sense of self.

My biggest lessons learned over time were to be gentle and kind to myself. I also had to learn how to deal with anger appropriately so that instead of lashing out at those closest to me (usually a boyfriend) or hurting myself, I could chose to turn that anger energy into something more positive. I also learned to choose my therapists carefully as not all were appropriate or helpful and each had a different style and personality. When I found a good therapist, I was able to learn to trust and open up. Interestingly, I made the most progress in dealing with sexual abuse issues with a good male therapist utilizing what is described as body psychotherapy. Later, I healed the most from loss and abandonment issues that all adoptees face with a female therapist utilizing a mix of body psychotherapy and Reiki healing.

Many years later, I am happily married with a beautiful child and I have reconnected with my adoptive family. This was only possible after years of professional help and getting to the point where I didn't need them to understand or support me. I found enough support without them and I became strong within myself and eventually accepted them as they were, even if they could never have given me what I needed. In the end, my adoptive father and brother did acknowledge the hurt they

I am 17. I was adopted when I was 10, but there were problems in the family so I was sent away to live in group homes.

I am now in foster care and the family I'm with wants to adopt me. I'm so happy, but I have to wait until I'm 18.

caused and I have chosen to move on and not be a victim. I have chosen to make my life what I want it to be and not dictated by the thoughtless actions of others many years ago. It has been an extremely challenging but honest and truth filled journey that included many tears and emotions ranging from one end of the spectrum to the other. In the end, the journey was worth it as I am now capable of having a healthy and positive relationship with my partner, I can chose who to trust - including myself, and I have much love and wisdom to give to my child.

Resources if you are experiencing sexual, physical, or emotional abuse:

The most important message is that sexual abuse is never the fault of the adopted child! When the abuser is an adult you trusted, you can sometimes trick yourself into thinking that what happened was your fault. **Abuse is never a child's fault.** If you have confusing feelings that perhaps you caused the abuse to happen because you wanted to be loved, remember all adoptees and every human wants love. There is nothing wrong with your need for love and warmth from someone else - but there is something wrong when an adult, who is meant to protect and nurture you, breaks that trust and hurts you by touching you sexually.

If the abuser is someone older than you but is not quite an adult, they can bully you into being submissive and being quiet about what they are doing to you. You need to speak up and tell an adult whom you trust about what's happening. If the adult you trusted does not do anything, then keep trying to tell someone until you are believed and are given professional help. The ramifications of sexual abuse left untreated can impact your life forever.

If you have suffered sexual abuse as an adoptee, please remember you are not alone! There are more of us than society wishes to recognize for all too often the story of adoption can be portrayed as a fairy tale where the adoptee is perceived to be materially "better off". However, when abuse occurs, no amount of material well-being can make up for the emotional and spiritual trauma that we are left to deal with for the rest of our lives. Adopted children are especially vulnerable and need protection and extra caution from being placed into abusive families.

What Worked for Me

READ *The Primal Wound* by Nancy Verrier. Everything I read in this book was like having a mirror image reflecting back at me.

CONNECT with a group of adoptees. This helped me turn my negative anger energy into something more positive.

READ *The Courage to Heal* by Ellen Bass & Laura Davis. This book helped me understand the impact of sexual abuse on my life.

SEEK OUT therapy individually and with a group of women who have been sexually abused.

VISIT http://www.eabp.org/ for further information on body psychotherapy.

The Queen Redeemed

Anonymous

She walks around the halls of her school with a little smirk. She has a sway in her hips and a jump in her step. One would think she is on top of the world.

Sometimes she actually believes it.

Why does she have this way about her? Because she's the queen. She's the oral sex queen. Her self-worth rises a little each time she is successful at pleasing a guy. "Other girls don't do it like you do," they say. "Some girls won't even think about it. You are the best." She smiles and gives that little smirk when she hears this, but what she doesn't realize is that each time she performs, the white liquid pours down on her soul and waters down her hopes and her dreams.

Her standards are washed away-until one day, she says to herself, "Why am I doing this? I hate this. I hate myself." She doesn't know who she is anymore. All she knows is that she no longer wants to be the oral sex queen. She doesn't know who she wants to be, but the thought of one more drop of that poison will kill any life she has left on the inside. No more. She can't do it anymore.

Years later, she looks back with disgust on her identity

as the oral sex queen. She thinks about what caused her to do that and be proud. . . connection, approval, success. . .she could do something that many others couldn't or wouldn't do.

What could have prevented her from serving in this humiliating role and the resulting hole in her heart? She could have realized that she would have done anything for connection and approval. Since the day she was taken away from her birthmother, her self-worth had been in the hands of others. Once she realized that she needed to take her self-worth back, she couldn't because of shame and guilt. She has had to walk a long road to forgiveness of herself, and now, she is on the road to happiness.

She's given her self-worth away again, but this time it's put into someone's hands who is worthy-God's hands. She is no longer the oral sex queen but a child of The King.

Why I Cut Myself

by Sadan Rollings

Hello. My name is Sadan and I'm from India. I am 17 years old and I am a student in my final year of high school. I was adopted with my older brother Madhu into a wonderful Australian family. We have mixed cultural backgrounds because six of the eight kids are adopted from three countries. I was around five years old when I was adopted.

I want to tell you about a rough stage I went through, because it might help people understand the challenges of young teens.

I was a happy little chap when I was young and I had heaps of friends. Before I came into my family I was a very shy and silent boy. I had not spoken at all for the two years I lived in an orphanage but I started talking soon after I joined my family.

When I was 13 years old I suddenly started being worried about things that hadn't bothered me earlier in my life. I had a girlfriend, and we liked each other a lot but we also got into arguments very easily. Sometimes I was really happy, but other times I was miserable, so I had a lot of mood swings.

I have always had trouble talking to people about how I feel. I find it hard to explain things. So, when I was feeling bad I couldn't really talk to anyone, and it built up inside me until I started taking it out on myself. I started self-harming. I would cut myself on my arms with razor blades until they would bleed, and sometimes I would cut again and re-open the scars when they started to heal. Most of the time I wore long sleeves, so at first my family didn't know I was doing this.

Cutting made me feel relaxed, and I would feel happier when I cut myself. It took my mind off other things when I would see the blood, but then the same worrying thoughts would return later.

I think my personality had to do with choosing cutting because I am quiet and I can't easily talk about feelings. I don't know if I was having these problems because of the things I experienced when I was a small boy or because of some of the challenges I faced with being adopted. Some of the pain was related to thoughts about being abandoned by my birthparents when I was around three years old. Those things came into my thoughts but it was also because of things that were happening in my life at that time – including bullying at school and being in love for the first time. Those things made me feel very vulnerable and insecure.

I'm not really sure how cutting helped me feel better, but it did. When I got into an argument with someone and I didn't get my way, then cutting would make me feel able to relax again. I don't really enjoy pain. The first time I cut myself it hurt a lot but then I quickly got used to it. It would actually make me feel better while I was cutting, and the physical pain from the cuts usually came later. I felt scared sometimes and that there was too much going wrong in my life. It made me feel stronger.

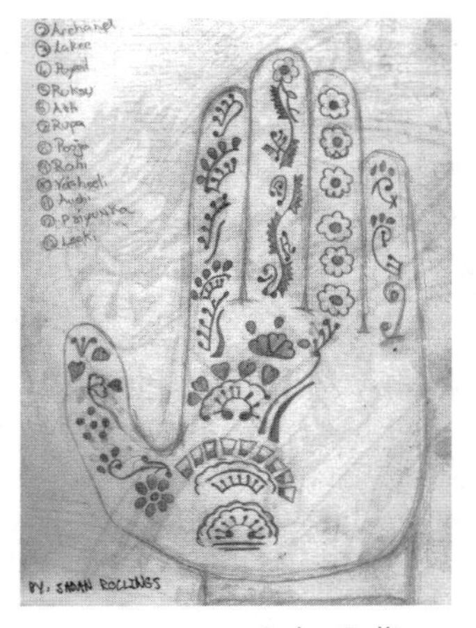

Sadan Rollings

Cutting made me feel that I was getting back at people I felt angry towards: my Mum, my girlfriend, sometimes my Dad, and some of the people at school. It would get back at these people because they got upset or upset by what I had done, so it made them hurt too. It was a way of showing that I was angry with the people who cared about me. It was also a way of pushing people away and making them feel bad, just like I felt bad.

The Test

Kim Eun Mi Young

We hurt ourselves
To feel alive
We hurt others
Because we must
Test
Always
Testing
To find worthiness
Of being loved
To find acknowledgement
That we are not worthy
Of love
We, who were
left in trash cans
Sidewalks
Hospital waiting rooms
Search always
for that first love

Eun Mi's other poetry can be found on pages 43, 53, 73, 121, and 148.

At this time I was also writing hurtful notes and doing violent drawings. I would leave these around my home where I knew my family would see them. I did this because I felt so much anger inside me. Doing these things made me feel stronger and in control. Once, I carved some swear words into my arm. Mum took me into her room when I came home from school and she told me to pull up my sleeve and show her my arm. She had heard what I had done from other kids at my school, so she told me she already knew about it. As she pulled up the sleeve of my sweatshirt I could feel her hands shaking. I felt happy because it showed me how much she really cared about me but also sad because I knew it would hurt her to see what I had done to myself. I did feel a bit angry towards my Mum but mainly I targeted her because I trusted that she would not leave me, no matter what I did – including hurting myself. Mum is important to me because she had raised me as one of her own, and I feel most comfortable around her.

My parents wanted to help me by taking me to see a counselor, but I did not want to do this. I eventually agreed to speak with my school counselor only, and I had several sessions with her. I also occasionally spoke with the youth worker at our nearby youth centre. I did it for two reasons: mainly because my Mum was pushing hard for me to do this but also as it made me feel a bit better. Now I am glad I did.

Talking to my school counselor turned out to be a big help. I don't think it would have worked talking to my parents at that time, because my parents were part of my problem. My counselor was able to talk about all the things that were bothering me, and that included my parents! The doctor wasn't any help, as all he did was tell me not to cut.

I don't really feel angry these days. I eventually started talking to people and they told me other ways to take my anger out, although I don't often get into arguments these days. I have changed a lot as I have grown older. I've learned to talk more about things and my relationships with other people are much calmer these days.

I think it is important to get someone to talk to a teenager who has problems. That might be a counselor, a brother or sister, or a family friend. Parents are sometimes too close to the problems or they are part of the reason a kid is self-harming, so I don't think talking to parents works well when things are going badly. However, it is important for parents to understand their kids. You must not give up on the kid, even when you can't understand them.

There is a lot I don't know about myself. I don't know much about my early life, and I don't even know how old I really am. Going back to India when I was 14 years old helped me to visualize how I used to live. When I visited my orphanage I was able to think about how things might have been if I had remained there. I learned a bit more about myself by learning a lot about India and where I came from. It made things more concrete when my family talked about places and events in my life.

Sadan, who is 17 years old, describes himself as "a happy chap"! He was adopted from India, along with his brother, into a large Australian family. Sadan enjoys music and art, and he hopes to work in childcare.

Being a Transracial Adoptee

By Deborah Collier

I am a 46 year old biracial woman. I have a white (English) birthmother and a black (Caribbean - don't know which island) birthfather. I was adopted when I was 10 days old by a white couple. This was back in January 1963, when transracial adoptions in the United Kingdom were arranged without much consideration for the cultural needs of the child being adopted. My adoptive parents were not told that it was important to provide me with positive black role models or to give me information on black history and culture. I grew up feeling English, but knowing that I did not look like an English child to people on the street.

The Narrative Burden (for more about this see page 116)

Not having information about my ethnicity was always very frustrating and a little bit embarrassing. The question when I was in my teens and as a child was always, "Where do you come from?" I would say "Staines," which is the town I lived in. This would be met with a look of confusion from the person asking. They would then have another go and rephrase the question, "No, but where do you really come from?" I would then have a bit of fun with them and say, "Oh, you mean where was I born?" Ah, finally a look of relief would come over their face. I would then say "I was born in Windsor" – this is an historic town in England and not a Caribbean island as the person asking was expecting! At this point most people would just shut up and leave me alone. But sometimes of course some fool would continue and just ask me straight out "Yeah, but where did you get your colour?"

At this point it was awkward because as an adoptee I don't know where my 'colour' comes from, and I would then have to explain my life story – that I was adopted but didn't know my birthfather. It made me angry that complete strangers felt it was OK to ask me the most personal stuff about myself and the only solution I ever used really to deal with this problem was just to hold my head up high and tell the truth. On being told I was adopted the response I got was always the other person apologizing and saying they were sorry. But then I got the last word in and would tell them they had no need to feel sorry for me because I had a really great mum and dad.

School and Racism

At my school there were about 1,000 pupils. There were two Asian girls and one Afro-Caribbean boy. That was it. I was surrounded by Whiteness/Englishness. Some of the boys at my school were racist. When I was 13 years old one boy refused to sit next to me in class because he was scared if I touched his pencil some of my 'black' would rub off on it! I didn't say anything to him or confront him; I just carried on talking to the other pupils as if nothing had happened. I didn't want to let him know that he had hurt my feelings. I thought if I ignored his racist behavior he would get bored and stop it. He gave me one afternoon of sheer hell making nasty comments under his breath so the teacher couldn't hear him but I just carried on with my work as if nothing was wrong. He did get bored and in the future would only make an occasional comment.

I would tell my adoptive mum when I got home that someone had made a racist comment to me. This was a big problem because as a white person she did not know what it felt like to experience racism. She knew that I was upset or angry, but could not realize how deeply humiliating it is and how it pierces your very soul. She had a little poem she would say to me, "Sticks and stones may break my bones, but names will never hurt me." She was wrong.

I had a teacher of English Literature, a middle aged white woman who often managed to make negative comments about black people in class. That takes some doing when you are supposed to be discussing Shakespeare's Romeo and Juliet! She also gave me bad grades in a subject that I was very good at. I took my essays to another English Literature teacher and asked her opinion on the grades the first teacher had given me. She was shocked that she had marked my essays with such low grades, but would not speak to her colleague to investigate.

I told my adoptive parents about this teacher's behavior, but without any personal experience they couldn't comprehend it. They didn't complain to the school or take any action. Fortunately, I was good at the subject and passed my exam in English Literature. I was angry that a teacher could be so unprofessional and discriminate against me, but also I was very frustrated that my adoptive parents could not understand what life is like for me as someone of a different ethnicity.

Looking Good as a Teen

As a young teen I wanted to experiment with my hair and make-up. As a biracial teen girl with white adoptive parents, my mum was unable to help me do my hair. My adoptive mum did her best and asked a friend that was a hairdresser to try and relax my hair when I was about 13 years old because I wanted to grow it. Well, it went straight but was a total pain to dry. My mum didn't have any hair tongs or fancy stuff like that. She would set my hair on old fashioned rollers and stick me under a hair dryer in front of the T.V. for about an hour until it dried. It was time consuming and the finished result was not all that great! It was only when I was about 18 years old I found a shop that sold products for black hair and could really make it look good.

As for make-up there were no brands I could find that did a foundation for anything other than a white complexion. It was a nightmare. Again my mum was unable to give me any help because our skin has different complexions. All of my friends were white since there were very few other ethnic minorities in my neighborhood. So I spent a lot of time and money buying different eye shadows and blush to try and find something that suited me. I did find products that I could use but I had to do it on my own and could never have a makeup lesson from my mum. I would look in magazines to try and find a model with features like mine to copy her style of makeup or clothes. It was rare to see a black model when I was a teen so that was also a real pain.

Family Silence

As a transracial adoptee, when you are with your adoptive parents you don't look like a family because you are not the same ethnicity as them. The adoption is always visible and your private life is always public. This is a trial. My adoptive parents never discussed this with me. They just carried on as if I was their own child and I couldn't and didn't talk about how this made me feel. I was with my adoptive mum at a party for young people and a woman that neither of us had ever met before just walked straight up to my mum and asked her if her hair had been curly when she was my age. I had a short afro hair style at the time; my mum's hair is straight. My mum just calmly said, "No, my daughter is adopted and mixed race." There was the usual embarrassed reaction from the person asking. Mum didn't say anything to me and we just dealt with these intrusive people by answering their questions honestly and then getting on with life. It would have helped me if we had sat down and talked about it. My birthfather's culture just didn't even figure in any conversations. I had no connection with my birthfather's culture at all.

So, I felt cut-off from my culture and in my early teens had no access to it. A solution would have been for my adoptive parents to find me books on black history/culture and take me to London where there is ethnic diversity, just so that I could see other black people. None of this was explained to them in 1963 when they adopted me. The overall struggle I experienced with my adoption is that my adoptive parents completely ignored my ethnicity and gave me none of my birthfather's culture. This meant I felt apart from both white/English culture and apart from my black heritage as a teen. As an adult I have visited several different African and Caribbean countries, had relationships with black men, and have educated myself on black history. It would have been a much better idea for follow-ups to be made on adoptive parents with transracially adopted teens to ensure they are being educated in their birth families culture.

Deborah Collier is a 46 year old dual heritage, transracial adoptee living in England. Because of her parents message that she was as good as the other (white) children at her school, she has grown into a confident woman despite many incidents of racism. Deborah has been accepted to sit on an adoption panel to ensure today's adoptees have successful placements.

copy this page (especially if this is a library book!)

Using this page, describe the piece or pieces that have been taken from you. What would it take to get it back? If you can't get it back, what can you do?

About a Boy

by Melinda M. Rosenthal

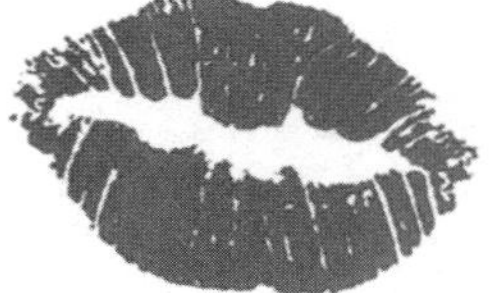

When I was 17, I fell hard for a boy. He was unlike any boy I had ever known before. Dangerous. He smoked too much, he drank too frequently, he cursed too easily, and he dabbled in drugs. Not at all like the well-mannered, God-fearing, line-towing boys from high school. Not at all.

And he was handsome, too. Full sensual lips and a devastatingly lopsided smile. Piercing blue eyes under perfect straight brows. Floppy brown hair. He was broad of shoulder and narrow of hip and every other swoony, stereotypical leading man description you can think of.

We met at a college dorm party. From the start, dorm parties and I co-existed uneasily. Alcohol affected me too quickly and too negatively. His first impression of me was hideous: me on my knees, puking into a toilet. He helped clean me up and put me to bed and never even made a move on me. The rational side of me thought, "How gentlemanly." The egotistical part of me wondered, "Why the hell not?" From then on, I was acutely aware of him.

Turns out he was aware of me, too, but not for the reasons I thought. He was dating a beautiful Chinese girl at the time, named Min.

Then he turned his attention to Mae, an incredibly smart Chinese girl with black hair flowing past her waist. She was so smart, she quickly brushed him off.

Then he turned to me, the remaining Asian girl in the dorm.

Then he turned to me, the remaining Asian girl in the dorm.

I was flattered by his attention. I had never dated anyone like him before. He exuded a confidence and worldliness far beyond my limited experiences. He was a Caucasian boy who had lived all over the Far East, including Korea. His father was a respected scientist with the World Health Organization. As a member of a well-educated, highly regarded Caucasian family living overseas, he was accustomed to being fawned over. He did what he wanted to do. He set his own rules. Girls lined up to be with him. Asian girls. He related very well to Asian girls.

In turn, I was an adopted Korean girl raised in the United States.

I grew up in an era where obliterating one's Korean heritage was standard. "You are American," I was told. "That's all that matters now." My Korean background was never discussed, never pondered. And so I morphed into a Caucasian girl trapped in Korean skin. I dated only Caucasian boys. The few Asian men I met didn't attract me at all. I was resentful when people tried to match me with them. What did we have in common, besides our superficial exteriors? Did people match blondes with blondes, solely because of hair color?

Our relationship deepened, and we fell in love. It came time to tell our parents of our decision to marry. My parents accepted him easily. He looked like them; he was well-spoken and charming, and they knew nothing about his dangerous side. His parents' reaction, however, blindsided me. From the other side of the world, in Burma (now Myanmar), they harassed him day and night about me. They told him I would ruin his life. They said if we married, his career would end before it started. Never mind that I was far more focused on a career than he was. I would drag him down anyway. They said Asians were beneath their social status. They claimed only blonde babies were beautiful. His grandparents chimed in, adding fuel to the fire, pleading with him to end it with me.

And this is when I learned of his dark underbelly, his hidden reason for being with me. To his family, our relationship was unthinkable because of my race; contrarily, his rebellious side reveled in flaunting my Asian-ness to them. If anything, I was not Asian enough for his purposes. He loved pitting us against each other. He reported to me, in excruciating detail, the hateful things they spewed about me. When they came to visit him, with his cherubic blonde stepbrothers in tow, they crossed my path often so they could pointedly ignore me. They stayed on campus for two weeks, and for the whole time they visited, we never spoke. And for the whole time they visited, he never defended me or our relationship. It was childish and hurtful.

If anything, I was not Asian enough for his purposes.

I had experienced prejudice before, but this was my first encounter with such overt hatred. I was honestly confused. I couldn't wrap my mind around why they hated me so much. In my mind, I was an All-American girl who happened to look Korean. I had no real sense of my Korean self; therefore, I had no real sense of why I was so offensive to them. I believed I was as capable as any other girl, Caucasian or not. I felt I was smart enough and talented enough to hold my own in our relationship. I couldn't understand what the fuss was about.

Of course the relationship sputtered and died. I grew tired of fighting his family. I no longer wanted to be his co-conspirator in a rebellion that I didn't understand. I couldn't reconcile being too White for him against being too Asian for his family. And as our relationship waned, he descended further into his dangerous dark side, sliding into the abyss of drugs and alcohol. When he started buying Guns 'n' Ammo magazine, it was time for me to leave. And so I exited, relieved, yet saddened, with the clarity of self-realization bestowed upon me. For a moment in time, I had been suspended between two cultures, neither of which I belonged to completely. It was only after this relationship that I fully realized my tenuous position in both worlds.

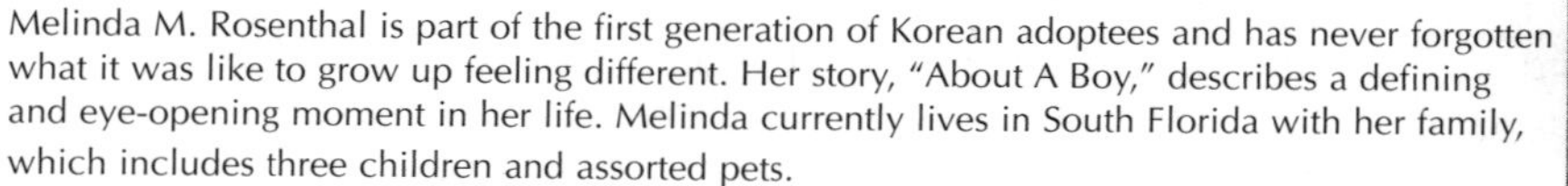

Melinda M. Rosenthal is part of the first generation of Korean adoptees and has never forgotten what it was like to grow up feeling different. Her story, "About A Boy," describes a defining and eye-opening moment in her life. Melinda currently lives in South Florida with her family, which includes three children and assorted pets.

Cost of Connection: My Life

by Angel Coldiron, LPC

How can I spill my heart out to you and you sit there in silence on the other end of the phone? You hear my heart crying out, and you don't seem to care. Why do I continue to lose myself in you over and over again? I know that our relationship is potentially fatal. All it takes is me setting you off one time too many, and my lifeless body would be laying there. The thought of "why did you allow yourself to stay in this situation?" crosses my mind during the last few seconds of my life. "Oh, my God, is this really how I am going to die? Not like this." How can I stay in a relationship that is so emotionally and physically violent? Why do I continue to put myself in harm's way? Why can't I just listen to my voice of reason? One minute I am ready to leave you, and the next I think I cannot live without you. Why can't I just be finished and move on with my life?

Why? It's because the loss of you brings up the emotions from every loss in my past—including the most entrenched of all—my birthmother. I cannot deal with the pain of the wounds that were inflicted when I was an infant. The wounds are too deep. The pain is too much. I am scared of what will come up if I allow myself to lose you. The cost of connection is a high price to pay, but I will pay it to avoid one more loss. Actually, it's not just one more loss; it's all my losses compounded into one because I have never let myself feel and heal from any of them. I have paid the cost of connection all of my life. I cannot stop paying now, even if the cost is my life.

Angel Coldiron is 27 years old and is from Jefferson, NC. She is a former foster child who was adopted when she was 1½ years old. She currently works with foster families and is a Licensed Professional Counselor. Her writings reflect her journey as an adoptee as well as the struggles of other foster children and adoptees she has met along the way. See another article from Angel on page 78.

What pieces do you wish you had back? Does that have to do with being adopted or something else?

Sandcastles and Waves

by Marni Denenberg

Life as a teenager is often described as "the best of times," but also confusing times. For the teen who is adopted, it may seem even more confusing. I was there, I know. I was adopted at birth. All I knew about my adoption was that it was a private adoption through a local lawyer and the hospital where I was born. My parents explained that it was a closed adoption and no identifying information about my birthparents was available.

Building Sandcastles I vividly recall putting on my makeup in the mirror and thinking ... "Who do I look like?" Keep in mind that I grew up in a loving family, with two parents, two sisters, a dog, cat, and fish. Regardless, I still had questions.

If I was unhappy or in a bad mood, I would daydream about my birthparents – what did they look like and where they were from? When I was angry with my parents, I would imagine a loud banging at the front door. It would be my birthparents coming to "rescue" me. Off we would go to live in a castle far away. All of my teenage worries and concerns would melt away and life would be "perfect." Arguments with my parents would usually end with me demanding: "I want my 'real parents'!" At other times, I would dump all of my possessions in a mound outside my bedroom door and sulk. I felt alone.

The Wave I searched for my birthparents as an adult. I was not looking to replace my parents, but still wanted answers. I needed to fill that emptiness I had been carrying throughout my life.

The phone rang. I was at work and expecting a call on a project. When the woman introduced herself from the adoption registry, my mouth dropped and I felt queasy. "Do you want the good news or the bad news?" she asked. The good news – they had found my birthmother. The bad news – she had passed away. No! I felt like I had been punched in the stomach. Tears welled up in my eyes as I listened to the information about Brigitte, my birthmother.

Two weeks later my birthfather was located. He was alive and living in the same state. We met for lunch. We talked, looked at some old photographs, and compared hands. He was full of personality: shark fishing, scuba diving, airplane flying, successful businessman. He was short, stocky and Italian. He had a wife and three children, who he referred to as my brothers and sister (they were really half-siblings, but whatever). He had a family of his own and feared telling them about me. At the end of lunch, we promised to stay in touch and he said he would tell his family about me "when the time is right."

It has been over ten years since that lunch and I remain a family secret. We speak and email on occasion and I feel happy to know him. But being a family secret is painful. It is.

Wash Away As you can see, finding my birthparents did not work out how I had imagined. All of my longing and daydreaming was just that ... a daydream. The waves have come and washed away the sand castles of my youth.

Marni Denenberg is an adult adoptee who has worked as a professional in the adoption field for several years. Based on her personal and work experiences, she hopes her writing will help teens view adoption from a larger perspective. Her personal adoption experience continues to unfold, and she wishes everyone peace and happiness on their own adoption journeys.

vanished like time

By Jasmine Renee Pyne

I miss you in all,
I want to recall,
I'm not feeling very tall
You vanished like time,
I stay in the line,
My heart is searching for you

I want to sob,
My heart does the job,
I'm hoping to finally find you
The time that we spent,
You came and you went,
It seems like it meant so much

But you vanished like time,
I stay in the line,
My heart is searching for you

Cry I shouldn't,
How I couldn't,
It's all a memory now
I want to sob,
My heart does the job,
I'm hoping to finally find you

You vanished like time,
I stay in the line,
My heart is searching for you
My heart is searching for you....
My heart is searching for you......
My heart is searching for you........

Jasmine Pyne is a
13 year old adoptee
who plays guitar,
sings,
and writes her own music.
You can hear her music at
www.acousticesp.com/Jasmine/Jasmine.html

white skin on my hands

By T. Reid

I'm not seeking validation or to make you feel bad
I just want you to know what a tough time I had
An adopted child you wanted to have
But at my expense I made you glad
I eased your mind, your responsibility
About raising a black child in a white family
You always told me that everyone is the same
Which stopped me from talking about all the shame
About being born black and growing up white
And how that was such a difficult fight
It's my time now to let you know
It's my time now, so here I go
I tried and I tried to ignore the feelings inside
But the thoughts that haunted me would not subside
So I did what I could to get through each day
Hating myself was not an easy way
So many nights I cried in my bed
Wishing these feelings were out of my head
You did not help me at all to understand
Why there was not white skin on my black hand
I longed to be free of thoughts haunting my mind
I longed to feel comfortable with my own kind
I hated my life, I hated it so

But there was nowhere else, nowhere else I could go
To the sky up above I looked and I said
Is there another family that could adopt me instead?
I wanted a family that could understand
A family to help me be all that I can
I tried to manage my feelings inside
But the thoughts were burning too deep to hide
So I turned to things that I am ashamed of today
To get your attention in any way
I longed for your attention, for you to understand
Why I wished for white skin on my hand
Today I am ashamed, ashamed to be me
But I am learning without you, learning to be free
It's still a struggle for me to understand
That it's ok not to have white skin on my hand
But there will come a day when I will be proud of who I am
There will come a day when eventually I can
Look in the mirror and not wish to be white
Look in the mirror and know I was right
That color does matter, it matters a great deal
And ignoring that fact helps no child heal

T. Reid is an adult adoptee from NJ who was adopted into a transracial adoptive family. She has struggled with adoption and race issues throughout her life. Her poem is about her struggles growing up as a transracial adoptee and not feeling that she could talk to her adoptive parents about how she felt.

twenty-seven

by Juli Jeong Martin

i don't mean to set parameters
what this can be
what it isn't
or claim the common language of loss
to be universal
but in my wayward orbit
weaving kamikaze missions against
brick walls of what some say is truth
this is where i always return
this is where the convex fits concave
& when the heads of scholars shatter
i will stretch these simple words
to build my home.

so this is how i choose to talk to you

there is so much i do not know
but want to claim as owned by me
owed to me
there are landscapes i want to etch
behind my eyes
& native tongues i wish to colonize
there are flavors that i seek to hold inside me
& sounds i hope to melt into my veins
there is a country & a people
i need to want me back

but where is my birthright?
was it surrendered like citizenship
discarded as a burden
that would keep me from moving forward
because you can't look back
if there is nothing there to see

still i am looking back
but am trapped by my reflection
because you are a part of me
not an incandescent apparition
or vapors curling from an unknown past
no, you remain something i can't see
with these two eyes that are your own
you are hidden beneath the surface
every cell saturated, &
the marrow, the very pith of me
filled with the fiber of ancients

maybe that is why
i always tried to take myself apart

because when i look at me - you - me
i see solitude
even though in every direction
i am one of many
those lineages are contested
& maybe that is why
i dress myself in difference
so that i can see myself in someone else
& feel included in the family i have made
constructed yes
but is it any less true than others i have known
& does it even matter

i surround myself in noise
to drown out the silence
i surround myself in noise
to drown out the silence
to
drown
out
the
silence.

Juli Jeong Martin: queer korean adoptee, poet, artist, performer, organizer, mover, shaker and misfit. skilled vegan chef, aspiring zinester, crafter extraordinaire and sometimes drag king. She is the founder, editor of Grinding Up Stones: The Asian Adoptee 'Zine
grindingupstones.wordpress.com
Find more of Juli's thoughts on pages 28, 47, 122, and 142.

Two Worlds

By Kim Eun Mi Young

What can you say to us
The "chosen"
The lost children
Of birthmothers
Too wounded, too young, too selfish
To care

What can you do to lessen the pain
The rejection
The anger
The knowledge
Of trash cans and city steps
Orphanages and foster homes

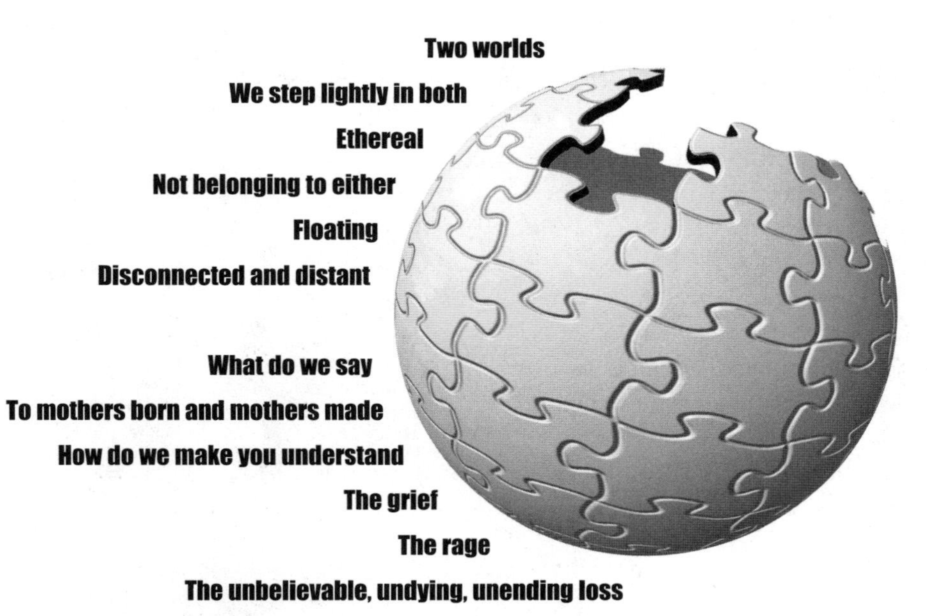

Two worlds
We step lightly in both
Ethereal
Not belonging to either
Floating
Disconnected and distant

What do we say
To mothers born and mothers made
How do we make you understand
The grief
The rage
The unbelievable, undying, unending loss

Eun Mi's other poetry can be found on pages 43, 53, 60, 121, and 148.

Born Running

by Lisa Dickson

When he asked her why she was running, she looked at him in surprise.

"I was born running," she said, tossing her head, as if there could be no other explanation.

And, the more she thought it over, she could see that she was. Running from a mother who died, who left her. Running from a father who had never loved her, who abandoned her. Running from a man who raped her, from boys in high school who took her places that she never wanted to go.

"I was born running. And I do a damn good job."

He wasn't shocked at her response. Didn't lift an eyebrow at her language. Just smiled an easy smile, unlike any man had ever smiled at her before. His hand on her shoulder was gentle, to match the soft tone of his voice. "What are you running from? And why don't you stop?"

She could think of no possible way to answer him, so she turned on her heel and walked away. Who was he to care about what happened to her? How could he know anything about the situations she was dealing with? Why should he care?

Still, the question, at the least the first one, reverberated in her consciousness. There was no way of stopping – but could she name the demon? What was she running from?

Later, it came to her. She was running from the shadows of things left behind.

Lisa Dickson is a former foster child and current youth advocate. Her passion is improving outcomes for young people "aging out" of foster care. She is involved in Ohio Reach, an effort to improve college enrollment and graduation rates for foster care alumni.

POSTCARDS FROM THE EDGE

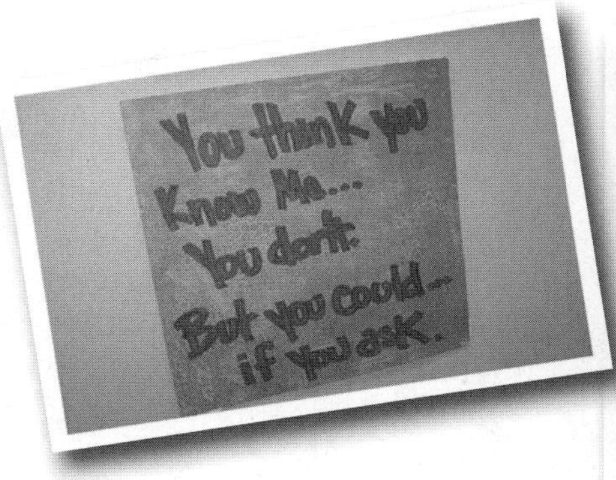

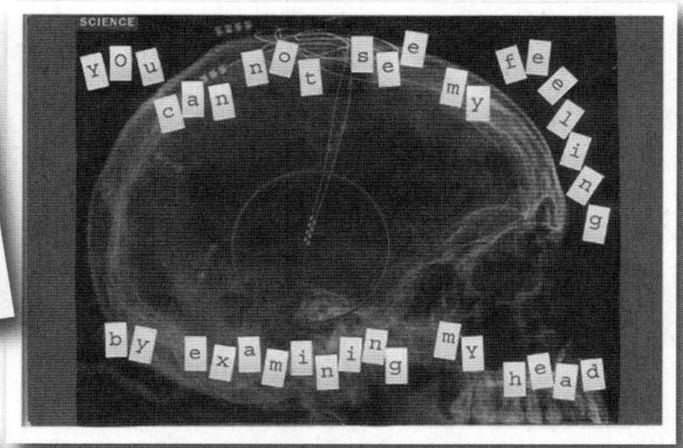

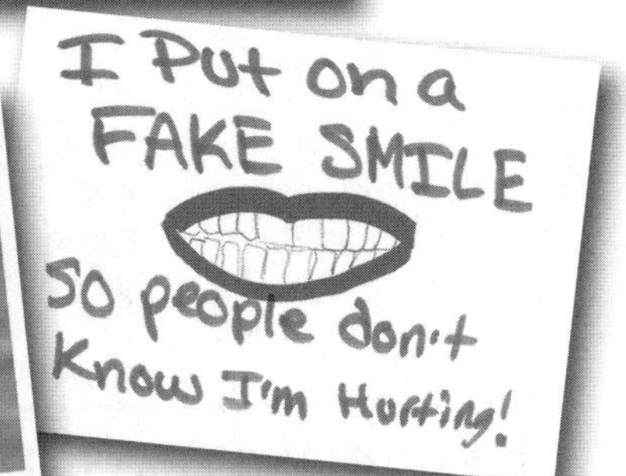

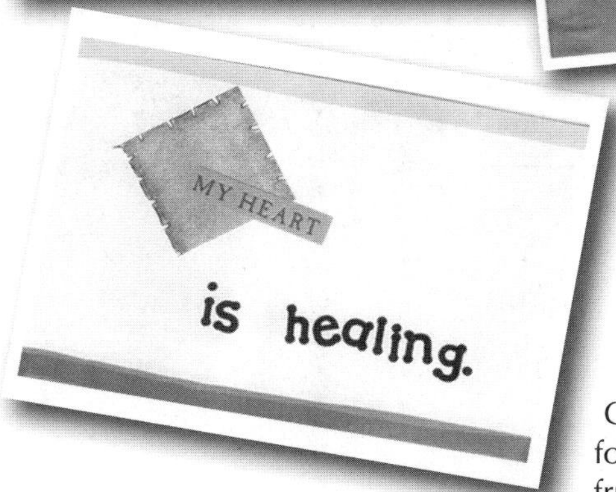

Have you ever wanted to express how you REALLY feel about something in your life? Have you ever wanted to write down what's really going on with you?

Here's your chance!

Called Postcards from the Edge, this is an opportunity for you to write down, sketch out, or draw your anger, frustration, grief, or sense of loss at what's been stolen from you. Or, an opportunity to express your joy, happiness, contentment, excitement, or whatnot at something that's happening in your life. If you want, when you're done, you can send it off . . . or maybe just post it on your wall or put it in a special place to revisit another day. Maybe even send yourself a postcard as a kind of pick-me-up or reminder of what you felt a few days or weeks ago. Check out these examples by some foster care alumni and get to designing your very own postcard! There are no rules . . . and you can do it as many times as you want! If you are a foster care alumni, there is a special place you can send them as well. Turn the page to find out more!

Are you a foster care alumni?

You are invited to contribute to a group art project of the community of foster care alumni in the US and internationally. We are exploring the culture we all share—the culture of foster care—by sharing experiences, insights, and what we've learned. We will be posting the cards on our website at www.fostercarealumni.org and are also planning to develop traveling exhibits of the cards for use at conferences, training events, and other public venues. This project is intended to build the alumni community at the same time we educate foster care professionals and the general public about our culture.

INSTRUCTIONS:
Create your 4-by-6-inch postcards out of any mailable material. If you want to share two or more messages, use multiple postcards. Put your complete message and image on one side of the postcard, the address below goes on the other side.

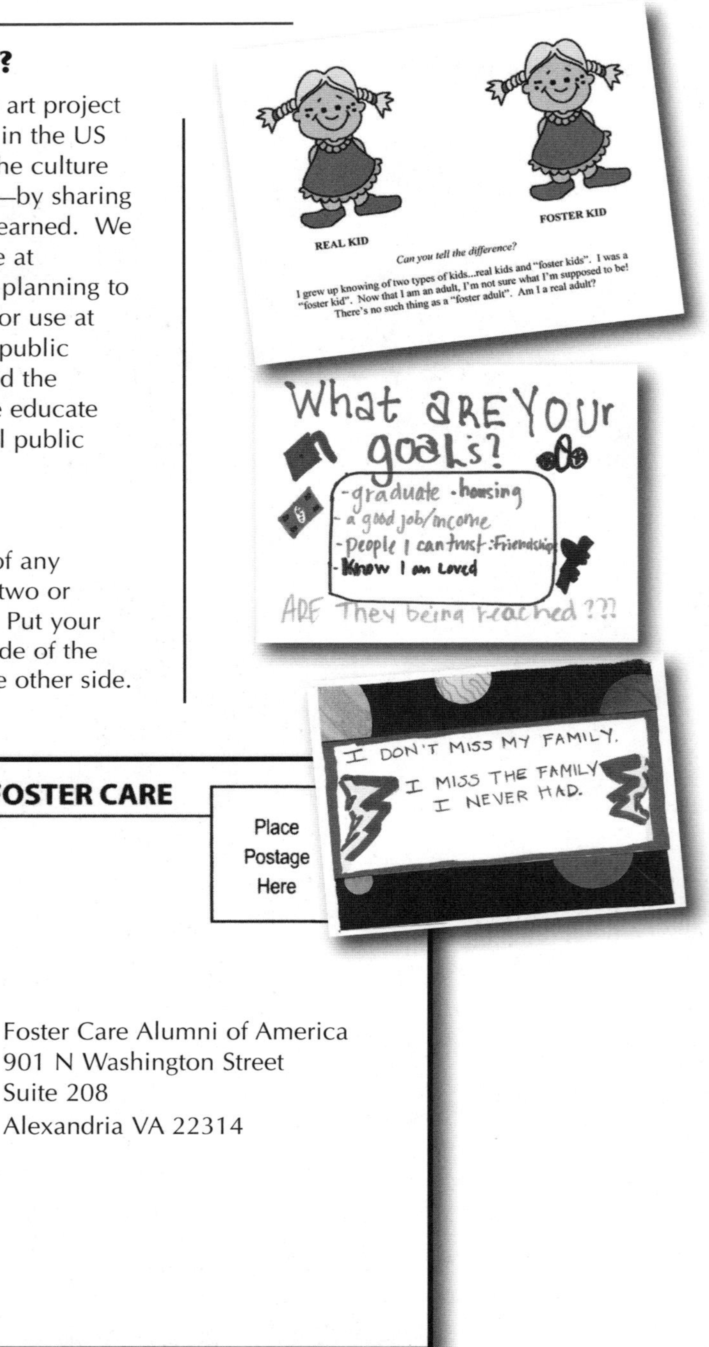

EXPLORING THE CULTURE OF FOSTER CARE

You are invited to contribute to our alumni community group art project. We are exploring all aspects of the culture we share—the culture of foster care.

STEPS:

- Use this postcard or any other found or made card.
- Customize your card by sharing something about yourself, your experiences, or your life that is connected to your status as an alumnus of the foster care system.
- Stamp and mail your postcard.

TIPS:

- Be brief and legible.
- Be creative—let the card be your canvas.
- Share the idea and the opportunity with alumni every chance you get.

Place Postage Here

Foster Care Alumni of America
901 N Washington Street
Suite 208
Alexandria VA 22314

Fitting the Pieces

The fun part of any puzzle is when something fits and makes sense. There is a moment of euphoria, a high to when we finally figure out where that piece goes!

So it is with *Pieces of Me*. When we figure out where a piece goes, it feels really good. We feel a sense of relief, a sense that all of it fits! Yes! I'm figuring me out! I'm figuring out who I want to be! Even though I don't know everything about my life, I'm still fitting it together, somehow, someway.

That is something to be proud of.

That is what this section is about, about people who have fit the pieces into who they are and who they want to be. They've taken the stolen pieces and figured out how to fit them in. They've made adoption a part of their everyday life. They've fit birth-parents and birth family into their lives in meaningful ways. They've learned to live with loss.

These are not perfect people. Their puzzle isn't complete. But at least they've placed a piece or two or more. They at least have made a connection and have seen part of their whole.

Come and see how pieces can fit together.

The Lifelong Journey

by Angel Coldiron, LPC

As an adult adoptee, I often quote the title of Maya Angelou's book *Wouldn't Take Nothing for My Journey Now* because I now understand the value of the journey of life. Where I have been and what I have gone through has made me who I am today—the beautiful pieces of me that shine and the hidden pieces that only rear their ugly heads when I can no longer manage them under the surface. All of these pieces are a part of me. I have some pieces that have rained down from heaven. I have picked some shattered pieces up off of the floor. I have some pieces that have come from explosions of anger and some from implosions of depression. I have been given pieces from family members that I did not know what to do with—so I put them on a shelf until I can figure out where they belong.

I am still putting the pieces together of who I want to be and have discovered that doing so is a lifelong journey—one that I "wouldn't take nothing for." I used to let others take my pieces and place them. Slowly, one by one, I am reclaiming the pieces of my life, and with God's help, I am putting the puzzle together to shape who I want to be.

We want to thank Angel for this contribution and also to her contributions for the Title Contest we held for this book. She helped us to create the winning title and won a red i-Pod nano. See another article by Angel on page 67.

I am a bastard

By Ned Levy

I am a bastard. Literally. An adopted bastard, fortunately for me. My biological mother was eighteen when the man who impregnated her disappeared into the night. I'm a little fuzzy on the details as I wasn't there at the time, and I've only heard one version of the story from one related party. But I did get a break, a HUGE one. I only wish upon every adopted child in the world the kind of love and upbringing I was afforded by the family (MY family) who chose me to be theirs.

And that's not to say that my real (adoptive) mom's parents and siblings were entirely in support of her adopting me as a single mother on a teacher's salary in 1982. But I would not know of their disapproval for many years, and to this day would NEVER have had any reason to suspect that they were anything other than supportive of this bold and selfless decision.

The part of my childhood that I can remember revolves around growing up in the beautiful mountains of Vermont. The air was so fresh that it gave you the feeling of being cleansed, especially after one of our trips to New York or Boston, where the air was acrid and heavy with the smell of bustle and business, rubbish, and (of course) that unique smell of 'street people.' Vermont. Home.

> I won't use being adopted as an excuse for the decisions I made, because no excuse exists.

My summers were equally, if not more impressive as the rest of my year. My grandparents lived year-round in a beach house on Cape Cod. There are so many people who never even get to see the ocean in their entire life, but for a good portion of my life, I owned the Atlantic (until my early teenage years I wrongly believed that we had been gazing upon the high seas of the open ocean). I would spend countless hours combing our beach, and all the other beaches I could walk to from ours, in search of the wonderful and mysterious items the sea had decided to give back to the land from which it came. Even more countless hours were spent hopping from rock to rock on the jetties, tempting fate and certain doom if I planted a foot in the wrong spot or just plain missed and fell. Somehow I never managed to crack my head open or break anything. I guess I was pretty nimble or pretty lucky. The air was clean here, too. Not crisp clean like Vermont. In fact, the smells of the ocean can be quite offensive to the unappreciative breather of air. But there's something about the briny, clammy air on Cape Cod that is just natural and right.

Ironically, my memories of how clean the air was in both Vermont and Cape Cod are marred by the fact that I have been smoking cigarettes more than half of my short life, which is only one of the many poor lifestyle choices I have made since my early adulthood. The significance of describing my wonderfully privileged youth is to emphasize the extent of my subsequent mistakes in life, and perhaps more importantly, the extent of the anguish I felt inside, which allowed me to rationalize these terrible choices.

I won't use being adopted as an excuse for the decisions I made, because no excuse exists. I will say that the fact that I was adopted and the circumstances involved may have played into the already significant and sometimes destructive anguish brought on by the dreaded teenage years. I started drinking alcohol and smoking cigarettes when I was approximately twelve years old. By thirteen I had caused such a ruckus that my mom was compelled to send me to a boarding school for 'bad kids.' By sixteen, I ran away from that school, got myself enrolled in my old local school, and then promptly expelled for assaulting a teacher. At seventeen, I was arrested twice in two weeks for DWI. The second offense resulted in an accident which nearly killed me. By nineteen, I was regularly using and selling hardcore drugs. My elementary school teacher mom was forced to believe that she had failed me as a parent, and had to turn her back on me for lack of the strength to watch her only child destroy himself. What parent has that strength?

But it wasn't the strength or lack of strength during this period which made it through to me; it was the strength and love she had shown me throughout my childhood that made me believe in my heart that she would help me back up again. And she did. Mom was living in New York State at this time, and I was still in the general Vermont/New Hampshire region. I was essentially homeless, and managed to keep shelter by couch-crashing from place to place until I wore out my welcome at each one. I finally ran out of places to go, and my mind, body and soul were worn thin from drug use, alcoholism, and sleep deprivation. On Christmas Day of 2001, my mom made the five hour drive from New York to once again save her son.

For the adopted child, no matter what age or what you are going through: remember that they ARE your real parents—they chose YOU. They loved you enough to choose you to be their child, and you can get through anything with their love and support. Don't take your parents for granted; you are their miracle, and they are yours.

Once I was in New York, my mom got right to work on nursing me back to health. I agreed (after much persuasion) to see a therapist and an acupuncturist. I think both men were more of a distraction than anything in the grand scheme of things, but I liked them both immensely. It was the hour-long drives to and from these appointments that made for prime fighting time between the two of us (at twenty years old, I still hadn't gotten my license back). We still had loads of unresolved issues, mostly stemming from my choice of lifestyle, and the car rides put us in close proximity for battle. We would later find that most of our festering resentment toward each other was a direct result of living under the same roof; it is still one of the biggest issues for us to deal with for more than a few days at a time. Once I moved out and became more or less independent, things started to look up for us.

There is no fairytale ending to this story. Nothing is ever perfect in life – never will be. At twenty-five years old, I still have ups and downs with my mom. In some ways, I'm still the blooming idiot I was when I was seventeen (I currently employ two attorneys; one for my almost completed divorce resulting from a six month long marriage, and one for yet another DWI arrest. How can smart people be so dumb???) I can safely say that none of our occasional battles have anything to do with being adopted, and there is absolutely no question about who my REAL mom is. Not to diminish the difficulty of pregnancy and childbirth, but any female can bear a child. It takes a MOM to change dirty diapers, to teach a child to read and write, to instill values of what is good and right, to resurrect a son who has condemned himself to the life of a vagrant scumbag.

It is not easy to be an adoptee, nor any easier to be an adoptive parent. At times, the pain for both parent and child will be entirely unbearable. For the child, questions will exist throughout their entire life: How might things have been different? Where are my biological parents? Why did they give me up? As an adoptee who has met one of their birthparents, I can say that there are still an unimaginable amount of these questions that will forever go unanswered. For parents considering adoptions: is adopting a child worth the Hell you might face to first get the child, and then raise him/her? If you ask my mom, she'll say "Absolutely. No question about it." For the adoptive parent having innumerable and hurtful difficulties with their child, will there ever be an end to all this? Almost definitely. Just keep loving your child and telling them that you love them; do all that you can for them and don't give up hope. For the adopted child, no matter what age or what you are going through: remember that they ARE your real parents—they chose YOU. They loved you enough to choose you to be their child, and you can get through anything with their love and support. Don't take your parents for granted; you are their miracle, and they are yours.

Ned Levy, December, 2007

This article was written by my son, Ned, in December 2007. He was twenty five, and searching for a way to start a career as a writer. When he e-mailed me this piece he said he hoped it "might help other kids and parents who have struggled the way we did." Ned died in a motorcycle accident three months after this article was written. I submit it in the hope that his wish might be granted.

The Proverbial Bag of Crap

Everyone has one.

It's full of all the crap that's happened to us that we don't like.

(Like people treating us badly, ways we've been hurt, families created without our choice, things we didn't want to happen to us but did, and so on.)

Each of us has to carry our own bag.

No one person's bag of crap is better or worse than someone else's.

Each day we have a new chance to figure out how to carry this bag of crap we have.

To deal with it or not to deal with it, to empty it or fill it, to put some of it in someone else's bag or let part of ours go.

What will you do today with your bag of crap?

The choice is yours...

Out On A Limb

by Josie Brett

I'm relaxing in my front yard gazing at the huge old tree towering over me. Its base is solidly rooted in the ground and as it reaches toward the sky, it has a prominent split that divides it in two, with each half growing in opposite directions. Above that, branches grow randomly as if reaching for the clouds. Oddly enough, I see much of myself in this tree. I too feel like I have a strong foundation, but now I feel like I am growing in many different directions.

Half of me still clings to the edge of childhood, while my other half ventures toward the cryptic world of adulthood. At 13, I am expected to be more independent, responsible, and reliable. On the other hand, I'm not quite ready to give up my endless hours of freedom and creativity, not to mention my bedtime stories.

My body feels like a stranger's, and when I look in the mirror, I don't know who I see. I must continue to grow, but I'm not so sure about my roots. I was born in China, but after being adopted, all of my growth has been in Colorado. I feel like my roots grow all the way through the earth, only to surface in my native land, so far away.

I have so many questions, but as I develop I hope these answers will fill in like the leaves on the tree. I'm not certain which directions my branches will grow or how my life will emerge, but change is good. I'm ready for new challenges, but I still have lots of frogs to catch, too.

This is a good time to be me! I think I will go out and climb my tree.

Josie loves writing her own stories and loves reading everything. She is 13 and a total Beatlemaniac. She has lots of fun playing the piano and the guitar with her sister. Someday, she will live near the ocean and have lots of animals.

Our Echo

by Amy Alejandra Silverbrandt

Cambodian legend states the Echo Room at Angkor Wat was designed specifically for setting free the suffering of one's heart from the simple act of beating on the chest. Facing a group of ten adoptees ranging in age from seven to fourteen, I watched them concentrate on their hands as they clenched their fists and drummed them across their chests. Our heartbeats leapt from our bodies and swirled upward, captured by Cambodian air

....Boomp, thump, boomp thump, boomp thump, boomp thump...

My personal story began a world away from Cambodia, in Santiago, Chile. Some unknown force deep inside of me must have changed my aching heart into a compass that was destined to direct me back to Chile when I was seventeen. As I took my first few steps in my birth country, I realized my feet had left, but my footprints must have always stayed. How else did I greet everything with such a comforting familiarity? Entering my family through adoption as a baby, my first flashes of being back in Chile transformed my curiosity, wonder, and hope, into another home. I knew that I had been officially born.

My job now takes me around the globe watching this feeling overcome adoptees of all ages. The transformation of self discovery for adoptees when entering their birth countries is not always easy or endlessly happy, but rather a distinguished truth that seems to have a unique and beautiful relationship with each of us. Even if an obvious truth is not found, such as the answers to our beginning, sometimes the simple act of seeing, can give an understanding that is the most healing.

I believe all adoptees are connected through our own universal echo room. We can empathize with the confusion that tries to bury the pain of losing a culture, a family, a language, a religion, and an identity. Together we can equally match the extreme privilege

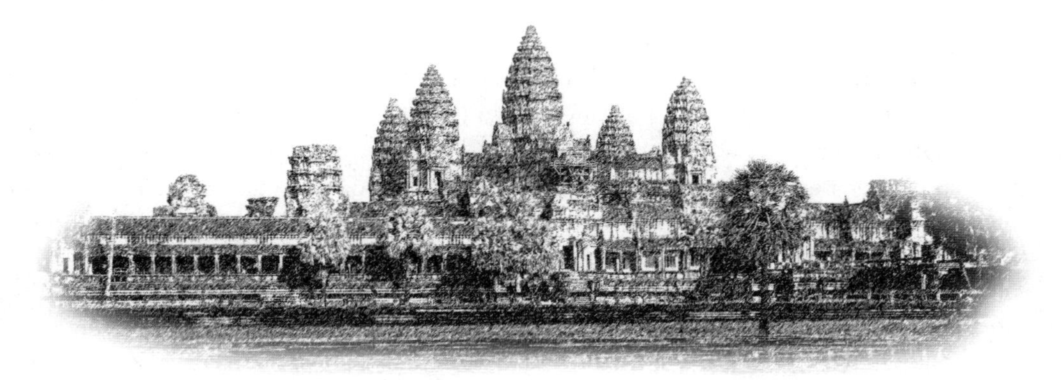

that we live with, as many times children from our countries of birth do not share the same opportunities as we do, which can leave an unsettling feeling of guilt and shame. However it is this echo that stems throughout the adoptee community, allowing us to communicate without any words necessary.

Heading back to the bus one day while in Cambodia, a girl ran up to my side reaching her palms up to my waist. "Please Madam," she spoke softly, "Only five bracelets for one dollar." Her dust covered cheeks and bare toes made me believe that my one-dollar might really extend an abundance of supplies to this tiny girl. I reached into my pocket to grab a buck and when I looked up, stunned faces circled me.

Even if an obvious truth is not found, such as the answers to our beginning, sometimes the simple act of seeing, can give an understanding that is the most healing.

Cambodian children had flooded our tiny area. Staring our Cambodian born adoptees in the eyes, these children asked, then pleaded, and then begged the adoptees in our group. Sometimes up to their shoulders with bracelets, postcards, or puppets to sell, it became obvious that there was more than one tiny girl that was in need of extra care in Cambodia.

As we drove back to the hotel a notable silence fell among the usual chatter that takes over the back of the bus. As we got off a hand brushed up against mine. I swirled around and found dozens of pairs of large brown eyes blinking up at me with one question I instinctively felt echoing through my heart, "Would that have been me?"

Sometimes the most adrenaline producing excitement is also the most terrifying. It is the small glimpse of reality found from being in your country of birth and realizing what your life might have been like, or could have been like. If we see beautiful people everywhere, does this help us see beauty in ourselves? And if so, what do we mean when we say beautiful? If we see poverty everywhere we turn, what does that tell us about ourselves? Does it offer any clue or link to why we may have been placed for adoption?

I believe that my soul weeps each time a child confronts me for money. The uneasy feeling that brews from our common human bond hurts me to my core while the adoptee inside of me balances guilt, thanks, and hope. I try to estimate all of the children in this world that do not have a loving family, education, or health care. I tell myself that I was one of them one day, but then ask why my lucky stars aligned and I was the "saved" child? Although very good intentioned, I have been told by family members or friends, "Don't worry, I don't see you like that. You are not one of them, don't worry." But what would be wrong with seeing me that way? That is where I am from.

Traveling to your country of birth may startle you at times. Sometimes the difference between your life and your birth culture vary drastically. Neither one is greater, more powerful, or more beautiful than the other. One of the greatest gifts I think adoptees can take away from visiting their birth country and heritage is seeing that no matter what possessions a person may surround themselves with, appreciating the pride that radiates from people everywhere on the globe is worth more than anything.

"They said it's not possible to find my birthmom," his hands cupped one another and he looked down.

"I know it's a really hard question to answer, but do you know if you would want to find them if you could?" Empathy flowed through me.

His eyes looked sideways, although I could tell they were searching for mine. They darted around until they fixated on a flattened Coke bottle sitting before us.

"I don't know how to hope for something that I fear is forever lost."

If you are not adopted I can see how it could be easy to assume all adoptees crave and plan a way to find their birth families. Although I do not believe this is a necessity for some adoptees, I think bouts of curiosity hit like the common cold, often unpredictable, and never one hundred percent curable. Whether frequent or rare, it is common for adoptees to build these thoughts on top of each other without sharing even one word of them. Confronting family members with these feelings can be challenging and scary, as adoptees tend to be protective of their loved ones. "I don't want my family to think that I do not love them if I tell that I miss, love, or want to know my birth family, or even my birth country." It feels like cheating.

Juggling back and forth between two very different worlds can be exhausting while exhilarating.

Last summer I spent a month in Korea traveling with adoptive families and participating in a few birth family reunions. After each one, the adoptees seemed to have taken the cast off of their fractured soul as they finally were healed. Yet a successful birth family reunion does not necessarily equal a "happily ever after." Not only does the adoptee have the opportunity to figure out what it means to be a son or daughter in another family, many times we are figuring out what it may mean to be a son or daughter in another culture as well. Juggling back and forth between two very different worlds can be exhausting while exhilarating.

Yet sometimes our stories can never be completed because there is no one to tell us about our first breath or our first cry. Others of us have memories of living in the countries where we were born, and our young childhood minds leave us with patchy memories and trying to fill in the gaps. There may never be a jackpot prize equivalent to finding birth family if that is what your heart desires, but hopefully you can find comfort in knowing that your longing echo is shared in our adoptee community.

After what seemed to be an endless number of hours in travel, the McIntosh family finally made it home to Memphis after their many days in Cambodia. Ready to wheel their suitcases inside and crawl into bed, their 10 year old daughter, Elizabeth, a Cambodian born girl, had other thoughts. Upon entering their house at 12:30 in the morning, she spotted a folded up Cambodian flag that has been there for years relatively undisturbed. She grabbed it up and exclaimed, "Let's hang up this flag right now!" So in the wee hours of the morning, after traveling 36 hours across the globe, she was running around the front yard enthusiastically waving the Cambodian flag before being lifted up by her father to place it in the flag holder on the front porch. And there her family stood, as the new day began, raising the Cambodian flag on their front stoop with a new pride never before expressed nor understood.

When I arrived home from Chile after my first trip at age seventeen I was no where close to being the same girl I had been eighteen days earlier. I knew down to my core that a difference had been profoundly ignited inside of my soul, as if all of my heart had been released, opened, and healed. I did everything I could think of to connect myself to my country. I slept soundly at night for the first time ever, as if calm had cast a spell over me. Refreshed and tranquil, for the first time I not only knew but could feel who I was – a priceless energy that still flows through my blood.

I think of my friend Elizabeth, and how she and her family gave life to their Cambodian flag which now waves proudly in the city of Memphis thousands of miles from where Elizabeth was born. What a symbol for this girl, showing the world that her roots connect to Cambodia yet her flag flies proudly in Memphis. She never has to choose or claim one over the other; she has been gifted with both. When I first heard of her excitement I could feel the echo of the same sensation I had almost six years earlier in Chile. Hard, nearly impossible to articulate, finding a point of connection is often the key to completion.

As adoptees we share similar roots of understanding and curiosity. Each one of our stories has been written just for us and no matter where you are, if you clench your fist and pound on your heart, your adoption heart song is echoed, felt, and understood.

...Boomp, thump, boomp thump, boomp thump, boomp thump...

Amy Alejandra Silverbrandt is a Chilean born adoptee with her undergraduate degree in social work. She travels with children and their parents embarking on adoptive family homeland journeys through The Ties Program (www.adoptivefamilytravel.com). Her role is "friend" as it is here. While traveling, she oversees "Connect & Chat" times with the kids as they are exploring their birth country, helping them process the incredibly powerful emotions & identity building messages a homeland journey brings.

Life isn't about waiting for the storm to pass, it's about getting out there and dancing in the rain...

Feeling Fostered

by Missy Kenny-Corron

There were weeks and weeks of newspapers piled everywhere with attendant chaos and mess. The refrigerator was completely empty and cobwebs were in every corner of the apartment. The Christmas tree was still up though it was probably 80 degrees outside and there were a few scattered unwrapped gifts under it. I remember that specifically because my marshmallow maker was under there, and I wanted desperately to open it up and start making marshmallows but, somehow, between Christmas in December and that day in June, it was never the 'right' time according to my parents. We had no phone, so I guess she must have left us alone in the house to go to the corner to call – or maybe she went to a neighbor, I honestly can't recall. Years after I heard her version of the day's events so many times I almost felt as if I had been there listening. "I called the police and told them that I would jump off the pier and take all three kids with me if someone didn't come right now and take them." "Them" of course was me and my younger brother and sister. I was six and the caller was my 26 year old mother.

"I called the police and told them that I would jump off the pier and take all three kids with me if someone didn't come right now and take them."

At some point that day some grown-ups (social-workers) came and in quiet voices they herded me and my two siblings out of the apartment and away from my hysterical mother. My mom always tended toward the dramatic, but she wasn't exaggerating. Things were about as bad as could be. My alcoholic father had disappeared weeks ago and without his meager earnings we were starving. I don't think anything else could have persuaded her that this was necessary but she also was too depressed to care whether we ate or not and that I think was the deciding factor.

After spending most of the day in a big office, we were summarily dropped on the doorstep of a house with nothing more than the dirty clothes on our backs. If anyone thinks that a six-year-old can not feel humiliated or shamed by circumstances beyond her control – well, you would be wrong. I felt it alright – had been feeling it since the moment those grownups walked into our filthy apartment and took us. We were introduced to some more people – and more than a few kids. Ranging in age from 18 months to 17 years the family had 5 children of their own and then we showed up. The family seemed nice and after the other grown-ups (actually more social workers) left, they put us in the back seat of a huge car and drove us to a toy store. We were given permission to pick one toy that we could have forever and that would be ours alone.

My brother, 2 years younger than I, had dragged his only possession with him, an old smelly brown teddy-bear; my sister who was barely 18 months and I had nothing. We walked up and down the aisles and to be honest, I don't remember what I chose – probably some ridiculous pink plastic thing. It really doesn't matter – what matters is that three dirty, scared, and friendless children were being given the chance to have one single thing that belonged to them alone. It was exactly what we needed at that moment. I don't know whether I loved my foster parents from that moment or one of the myriad that followed – but I know it was love.

Aunt Mary and Uncle Larry (as we called them) freed up one bedroom and stuck the three of us in there together again – the exactly right thing to do. Years later I would find out that we were only supposed to be there for 24 hours because after 20 years of fostering they had decided to stop accepting long-term placements and stick to emergency care. Apparently there was no one family willing to take all three of us so, they found three different families willing to take each of us individually. I think Aunt Mary must have known that would have been a disaster for us – she decided to keep us and keep us together.

"You have no parents, your Mom doesn't want you."

We endured a lot those four years. Taunts of our peers – "You have no parents, your mom doesn't want you." At one point my little sister became distraught, the result of neighborhood kids relentless teasing that she had no father, and so the social workers tracked ours down and forced him to make the one and only visit we got from him during the whole 4 years. We never saw him again after that day – and he subsequently died a few years after. Besides our mother, we had no contact with any relative at all during the time we spent in care. I know that at school I felt that the adults were all part of some great conspiracy – pitying us and offering cold charity when we needed it. Somehow, in spite of that we managed to do well.

One weekend four summers later we were planning to spend the weekend with our mother – who by then had been working and had a nice apartment. Lately, the overnight visits had increased so we didn't think anything amiss when she picked us up and took us to her apartment with small bags. Once we arrived she said, "Surprise! This is it! You are home! You are not going back to Aunt Mary and Uncle Larry's house!! We are back together as a family" I am sure a part of me was thrilled – but I also know that I was so darn mad! Furious even! I demanded she take us back right away since our stuff was still there, but it wasn't, all of it was in my mother's apartment. I don't suppose it was a coincidence but our foster family was planning a move to Florida and by the time we unpacked our little bags – our foster family was on its way to somewhere in Florida and we were never to see them again.

I cried for weeks at night – I couldn't cry during the day, I was aware of how that would make my mother feel – so I kept my feelings to myself. Crying only after I went to bed or during the rare moments I was alone. I felt betrayed and abandoned yet again. I wanted to go back to my foster mom's house – very clearly. We were happy there and with Mom visiting, it was the perfect arrangement according to my 10 year old rationale. Why would we want to live in the chaos that my mom represented when we could live in a nice house with a mother AND a father who was not drinking and hitting people; it was clean, had plenty of food, had other kids to play with and some semblance of normalcy. I have only happy memories of the time spent in foster care. Other than the embarrassment of being IN foster care – which other kids and sometimes grown-ups would inflict – it was still so much nicer. I adored my foster siblings. Most importantly, we were loved by the entire family AND our mom.

Over the years we came to accept the decision made by people we never really knew in offices far away. Our mom was great in lots of ways – but stability and security were never quite achievable and much of our life with her was one of scrimping by. I never for one second forgot my foster Mom. I would send her a silent thank you when someone praised me for an accomplishment – and while verbally thanking my mother I would harbor a secret that really I was the product of two mothers. Neither one could have been responsible for me alone – that is my mother started me – but my foster mother is the one that taught me to strive for excellence and achievement. I don't think I recognized that as being all that weird or unusual but I accepted it on some level because I rarely if ever spoke about it to my mother and certainly never mentioned that I had secretly wished we had been adopted by our foster parents.

Neither one could have been responsible for me alone – that is my Mother started me – but my Foster Mother is the one that taught me to strive for excellence and achievement.

What took longer was the resolution of the shame I carried as a former foster child. I took some pains for a long time to ensure that the conversation never took a turn in that direction. Like so many other previously neglected children I had a litany of things I felt shame over – alcoholic father, foster care, welfare, poverty, homelessness, a single mother and most of all the shame of disloyalty to my mom in feeling that my foster mother would have done a better job of raising us. Shame is toxic – in covering up my life I was living a lie in a sense, it wasn't until I was confronted with the choice to live that way forever or make a new decision that I finally came to terms with the fact that I was carrying around baggage that did not rightly belong to me. I had not made those choices – they had been made for me since I was the child. When, at last, I mentioned my four-year stint in foster care, I was surprised by the level of understanding and acceptance that others had. I mean, clearly people could distinguish between my own decisions and the decisions of those responsible for me. Today, it is a matter-of-fact item from my past, something that makes me who I am – but not the thing that defines me in anything other than the compassion I feel for the kids who are now struggling in some sort of care.

Eventually I looked up my foster family's name to see if I could get a phone number. I located a half a dozen names and numbers and thought, "Great! I will start dialing and maybe one of these will turn out to be right!" but when I reached for the phone I was hesitant and nervous. I was concerned that they might have passed on or that they wouldn't remember me. I held on to the numbers for a few years and in passing mentioned it to my sister. She immediately picked up the phone and dialed and we hit it on the first try. Sadly our foster dad has passed on the year before – but all the kids and our foster mom were fine! They had NOT forgotten us and were thrilled we are finally tracked them down and reached out.

We talked to our mom about it and she was happy for us and sent along some messages of her own. Mom was also able to express her gratitude for the loving care we received while she was unable to manage it herself. I was finally able to say thank you to Aunt Mary and get some of the missing information about how we had ended up with her family. I re-established contact with the foster sister I had missed most and with my Foster Mom.

Though life was often no fiesta with my mother – she did her best and there was never a moment that I didn't understand how much she loved me or my siblings. I suppose that is the reason it got complicated. I understood how much she loved us but I also knew that her love came with a price that was paid by her children. It was so much more uncomplicated with my foster mom. Though I know there were times I wished it had been easier – that there were no divided loyalties to sift through, I also know that I lived with these two women as my mothers all my life. I accepted that who I am in every sense of the word is a combination of both.

I am grateful in large measure because of the rocky road I have traveled.

I suppose that I could have turned out to be an angry person, full of resentments, regrets and endless "why me" questions. I am nothing like that! I am grateful in large measure because of the rocky road I have traveled and where I am is no place I could have dreamed of as a child. I also know that plenty of people discounted me and my aspirations on account of where I started – as if my ability to achieve was solely directed by the road I was traveling rather than the traveler I am. They were wrong to do that – it is not that important in the end how many mothers I had or fathers I did not have – rather it is important that I had people who cared at all.

I am now a mother to two internationally adopted children. My parenting approach is like my general approach to life – akin to filling a plate from a buffet table. A little from here and a little from there – all piled on one plate next to each other changing the taste and texture of whatever each individual item is – and creating something new and whole.

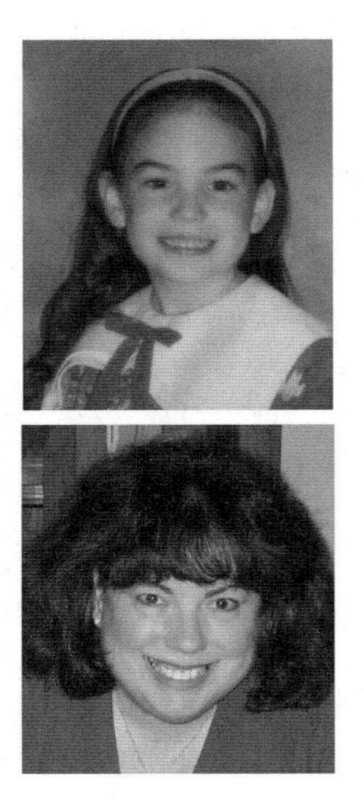

Missy Kenny-Corron was placed into foster care at the age of 5 with her two younger siblings for 4 years. Eventually they were returned to their mom. After 25 years Missy was able to locate and thank her foster-mom in person. She writes about her kindergarten photo at left, "looking at myself as a 5 year-old helped me to understand that NO 5 year old can be responsible for the choices that the adults in her life make. Recognizing that the 5 year old in that picture - my 5 year-old self was not bad or impossible to love... was healing on so many levels. "Missy and her husband live in NY with their two children – both of whom were adopted from China. Missy is an Assistant Dean at Stony Brook University – the same university where she earned her Bachelors in English Education and a Masters Degree in Social Work.

Which one of these is not like the other?

by Kelli Ann Smith

I don't look like anyone in my family. ANYONE! I am a kind of short, very chubby brunette. My family is the exact opposite! All the women in my family are svelte and blond. I look like a weeble wobble next to them (in my mind anyway.) The fact the I don't look like anybody I love really bothers me. I haven't ever told anyone that. Now, as I am writing this, I am realizing that it still bothers me.

I always knew I was adopted. I always knew who my birthmom was. I simply had never seen a picture of her. When I was 13 my parents told me that I could meet her if I wanted. I wanted to!!!!! I was so excited. So many thoughts and questions were running through my mind. The biggest being, "Would I finally find someone I looked like?"

Well, the big day came. I dressed very carefully. I wore my favorite purple shirt and jeans. I had my mom french braid my hair. I had longer hair at that point. I even put on some lip gloss. As I fastened my earrings, I was thinking to myself about what the day ahead would bring. We all piled into the car. My entire family along with all of our stuff. We were in the middle of a cross country move. Our car was packed, and I was nervous. It was a beautiful day in Washington. Sunny, but not too hot. Perfect weather! In the back seat, my sisters were behaving. They seemed to understand that this was a huge and monumental day for me. We made the short drive from our hotel to my birthmom's place. The butterflies in my tummy had joined the circus it seemed like.

I walked up the steps with my family in tow. I knocked on the door. The seconds before the door opened seemed like an eternity. My heart was pounding... BOOM, BOOM, BOOM. Then the door opened. There she was. We stood there completely gobsmacked for a minute or two. It was like looking into a mirror. I was the spitting image of my birthmom. The shock wore off and we hugged each other. The hug lasted forever. I stepped back and introduced my family. She introduced me to her boyfriend. We all trooped into her apartment. I was still wide eyed, trying to take in that I looked like someone. We have the same nose, same eyes, and the same chin. Our cheeks are the same chipmunk cheeks. Even our eyebrows are the same. I LOOKED LIKE SOMEONE!

After we got comfortable with each other, my birthmom pulled me aside and said she had something to show me. She took me back to her bedroom. All over her walls were hats. This is what she wanted to show me. I remember gasping. I had a hat collection too. We even had some of the same hats. I had never told her about mine and she had never told me about hers.

This was a life changing moment for me. Not only did I look like someone, we liked the same things! I was finally blending in! I had waited 13 long years to fit in. In the most unlikely place is where I felt an amazing connection, I fit.

Although I have never seen my birthmom in person again, I can remember that day so clearly. Since I have met her, I have also met other members of my birth family. We all have the same facial features and body structure. I take great comfort that I fit in somewhere and that I look like someone.

Kelli Ann Smith was adopted at birth. She has an open adoption with her birthmom and birth family. She is also a birthmom to two beautiful boys. She is married to her hero, a soldier in the USAF and is enjoying life. Her website is www.msbirthmom.com

Happily Ever After

By Maisie Howard

I felt alone like a stone
Like a piece of grass without a home
With no other love to discover in life
And the pain of every slap of hate
But that was all before
I prayed and prayed and a spark appeared
A new life started
Filled with joy and adoration all around me
With all the love I had, I thought my life was happily ever after
Like the fantasies I had been told

But it didn't stay that way for long
Days are going faster without a doubt
Struggles are popping up out of nowhere
Jealous of others and thinking they are perfect
Stressed from doing chores and homework
Having siblings bugging me and making the day worse
Dealing with friendship at school
People asking me if I was adopted
Every word someone says matters
Whether it's hurtful or something good
Whether they said it on accident or not
Because that shows what they really feel

When pressure comes it's like I'm locked in a room
Where there's no door or windows
Stuck in the darkness where I can't see myself
I have to make the right choice or I will be trapped with an unhappy ending
From time to time I fear I'm not a good person
Or maybe I'm a brat
But no matter who I am
My life is not going to be exactly the way I want it

Every day isn't perfect, but sometimes the struggles lose their strength
Even now I feel so lucky to be chosen by a loving family
I don't know what or where I would be if I weren't
Sometimes I feel my family is annoying
But inside me I know I still love them
And they are a part of me and my life
I'm no longer alone like a stone
I have lots of time to write my story

Maisie Howard was adopted from China when she was 8 years old and lives in Seattle, WA. She has an older sister and a younger sister who were also adopted from China. She enjoys dancing and creative writing.

Ben

By Benjamin Svetlozar Anders

I was adopted from Bulgaria on September 11, 2001. For many people this was a sad day, but for me it was my beginning. I am the youngest of five children, and I am the only one that is adopted. My skin color is also different from the rest of my family. Sometimes this makes me feel different from my brothers and sisters. When I first came here some people asked why my mom is white and I would just tell them that I was adopted. Nobody asked any more.

Even though I feel different, it is much better here than at the orphanage. I have a family that loves me and takes care of me. I can play sports and go to school. I have a family to spend holidays with. I can travel with my family to places I would have never seen before. I go to sporting events and hunting with my brothers. I have friends that I spend time with and we just have fun. My cousin is also adopted, but we just don't talk about it very much.

> My cousin is also adopted, but we just don't talk about it very much. . . . Most of the time I feel like a regular kid with a family of my own.

I used to dream that I would have to go back to the orphanage. I would dream that police would come to our house and tell my parents that I had to go back. It would make me feel very sad and scared. I didn't want to go back. I know that I will never have to go back now. I'm afraid that if I go back to visit they might make me stay. My brother, mom, and sister are police officers so I know that I am safe and will never have to go back.

I really don't think very much about being adopted. Most of the time I feel like a regular kid with a family of my own.

2008 Becky Orf Photography

Ben Anders is fourteen years old and lives in Bowling Green, Missouri, with his family. He was adopted on September 11, 2001, from Bulgaria. Ben was adopted at the age of seven and is the youngest of five children. He loves to play sports and can't wait until he will be able to drive.

Heritage Poem

By Kaitlyn Kraybill-Voth

My beginnings are lost
A shadow swallowed by distance and time
It is a candle
And the smoke is drifting away.

Mirrors reflect
Time
As the moon reflects
The sea
With the water that cradles
The soft particles of light.

I look at my reflection
While lines of time
Mold my face from her own.

From the silky raven locks
That fall down our narrow shoulders,
To every dark eyelash
Clinging to the slim almond eyes we share,
Even a feather floats in our fingertips.

A hand on my shoulder
A hand I never knew
A hand that touched a midnight rose
And laid it against my cheeks.

Her sky set to me in pinks
But the sun never faded away
Only I her child,
And she the mother bird,
Sent me into a new horizon
To fly.

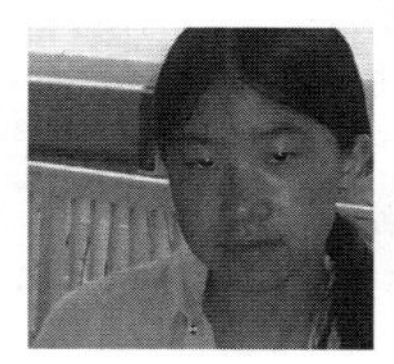

Kaitlyn Kraybill-Voth is 14, lives in Colorado, and hopes to become a Marine Biologist. She feeds her passion for writing through poetry. She understands that the pains of her past make her more susceptible and resilient to the inevitable adversities of the future.

Finding Rest in an "Adoptee" Culture

by Sarah Ballard

My name is Sarah. I'm not an adoptee, but I married one. We've been married for over ten years now. I also grew up with one brother and three sisters who were adopted from Korea. On top of that I'm a professional counselor and spend much of my time working with families and kids for whom adoption is a part of their story.

One of the most common statements I hear when talking with adoptees of all ages about their narrative burden (see page 116) goes something like this: "I am tired of looking / being different. Even when people aren't making fun of me, they are always asking me to tell them all about myself and how I got here. Sometimes I wish I could just blend in like everyone else." If you are reading this, I bet you might be able to relate to this statement.

"I am tired of looking/being different. Even when people aren't making fun of me, they are always asking me to tell them all about myself and how I got here. Sometimes I wish I could just blend in like everyone else."

In fact, you've probably asked yourself the question, "Where do I belong?" This is a hard question because sometimes the answer seems to be "Nowhere" or "I don't know." You might think, "I don't really look like the rest of my family, but my biological family has chosen not to keep me. I am neither a white American nor do I understand the culture of my birth country." Either way, you feel like you don't fully belong in either culture.

But there's a different way of looking at all of this. This way suggests that there is a "space" in between one's adoptive culture and one's birth culture. This space answers the question of belonging by saying, **"You are neither and both at the same time. You are an adoptee, and you occupy a cultural place that is unique and distinct."** In this space, diversity is the norm and no two families are the same, be it the family's religious or racial background, whether they have a single parent, gay parents, or a heterosexual couple for parents, whether they have biological, adopted, or no siblings. What bonds people together in this space is that as adoptees, it means they have a culture all their own. This culture is not completely their birth culture and is not completely their adoptive culture, but a mixture of both.

Why is this an adoptee culture / adoptee space important? In this space, I have seen adoptees, time and again, find rest from their cultural confusion and questioning. When many of the adoptees I know and talk to find a place where they can interact with other adoptees, they find that their struggle is lightened because when they are with these people they don't have to tell their story or explain how they feel. Other adoptees already know all the answers to the questions most people are full of. And other adoptees know what it is like to feel in between two cultures. They have felt what it is like to grow up in a family who looks nothing like them. They have felt the uncomfortable feelings every time they walk into a new situation wondering how long it will take for their unique story to become the center of attention. They know what it feels like when they become seen as "the adoptee" rather than all of the other good things about them. They have felt like outsiders and are just as eager to talk about, think about, and do other things as you are. Even still, when adoption does come up, these other adoptees don't have to wonder what that would feel like. They know. And somehow, that is very comforting. In this space, you don't stand out anymore. You're like everyone else! Everyone kind of already knows your story because they've got a similar one. All of this can be a rest from the struggle of where you fit culturally.

When you gather with other adoptees (or adoptive families) you find yourself in that space that is unique. You find yourself in that space with other adoptees who understand your struggle and confusions. In this space, as adoptees, you can make the burden lighter for each other. And, if you are willing, you might make some good friends you can hang out with. Or some lifelong friends. Or maybe your parents will begin to understand you a bit differently. Or maybe you will have a magical connection with another adoptee. Whatever the outcome, all of them are okay, and all of them can help to lighten your load a little bit.

In this space, as adoptees, you can make the burden lighter for each other.

Before I let you go, I want to make one more comment about connecting with other adoptees. It can be a wonderful thing, but you don't have to do it. It can help lighten your struggle and relate to others who understand. But even in the adoption world, there are lots of different people. Just because someone else is an adoptee doesn't mean you have to be their best friend or even their friend at all! And don't let your parents pressure you into having to do it! A lot of parents mean well and will take every opportunity they can to set you up with other adoptees, but I know some adult adoptees who never really connected with other adoptees in their youth and still don't today. Sure, they deal with finding a cultural home or space, but they don't see it as heavy a burden as some or have found other ways to deal with it. On the other hand, I know adults and teens for whom the struggle is very heavy and who need to have connections with other adoptees. Whatever you feel, wherever you're at, it's okay because in this "space" of adoptee community everyone is unique – not only in your backgrounds but also in how you decide what adoption means to you!

Sarah Ballard is proud to be married to Bert, the editor of this book! She has been a counselor for families touched by adoption, is the mom of two beautiful biological daughters (pictured here), and eagerly awaits news of a son from Vietnam. She feels deeply privileged to have been invited to journey with Bert, her many adoptee friends, her clients, and soon her son. She hopes that what she writes reminds you that, while all of our journeys are unique, we do not have to journey in solitude. Many others are on the same path.

I Just Missed You, That's All

By Patricia Dischler

Sometimes, it really stinks to be the grown up. We have this uncanny ability to over analyze everything! It was this drive to question everything, and read into actions motivations that don't exist, that lead me to one of the biggest misinformed moments of my life.

When my birthson, Joe, was 12 he asked his adoptive parents if he could meet me. We had an open adoption and had been exchanging letters and photos for years, but this would be our first face-to-face reunion. While I was overjoyed to hear the news, and quickly helped to make the arrangements, the little voice in the back of my head started to badger me with questions: Why does he want to meet me now? Is he going to be mad? Is he going to drill me on my decision? Is he mad at his parents and using me to get away from it? Is he not happy with them and wish he were with me? Or, is he coming to tell me that he wants nothing to do with me ever again? The questions surged and swelled, taking my anxiety on a ride with it until I felt like I was drowning in them.

Our initial meeting was everything I had hoped for: lots of hugging, crying and "I love you's." After the short first visit, we agreed to gather again the next day at my parents' house where they could meet the rest of my family. That evening the questions and anxiety began to build again as I realized Joe and I never really had any moments alone during that first visit and maybe he was just waiting until then to spring it all on me.

The next day he came with his parents and we spent the day pouring over family albums and sharing stories. The questions in my head were drowning out the conversations and I decided it was time. I asked Joe if he'd like to take a ride out on the river on my wave runner so we could be alone and talk. He agreed eagerly, which only raised my sense of dread. When we made it to a sandbar, I pulled up and killed the engine. I turned to sit off the edge of the seat, and so did he. I took a deep breath and dove into the unknown by asking, "Why did you want to meet me?" I braced for the questions, the accusations, the anger, and that loaded little word "Why?"

> *"My Dad read me that letter you wrote me in the hospital. You wrote 'I love you' in it a lot and I just figured anyone who loved me that much I ought to get to know."*

To my surprise, Joe shrugged innocently and answered "I just missed you, that's all."

Stunned, I decided he may just be scared to get started, so I gave him another opportunity. "Is there anything you wanted to ask me?"

Joe shrugged again and looked into my eyes. The honesty in them was unmistakable. "My Dad read me that letter you wrote me in the hospital," he said, "You wrote 'I love you' in it a lot and I just figured anyone who loved me that much I ought to get to know." That's it. No hidden agenda. No demands for details and over analyzed answers. Just a boy who knew someone out there loved him and was curious enough to get to see who it was.

In that moment I cursed being an adult. Assuming he had an agenda almost killed the experience for me, and I wasn't about to let that happen. I put aside all my assumptions and just listened. Joe went on to talk about how he had always wondered about who he looked like, why his eyes were so dark, why he had a dimple, and if there was anyone in this world that was like that too. I exchanged a caring look with my own dark eyes, smiled big so the dimple would show, and assured him he looked very much like his birth family.

When we returned to the house my Dad, otherwise known as Papa, was getting out his dulcimer and called Joe over to show him. Joe's eyes lit up and he ran outside, returning in moments carrying a guitar! His adoptive father turned to me and smiled saying, "So that's where he gets it!" We watched together as Papa, and a young version of him, began a duet of "Hymn to Joy." Joe's Dad turned to me and said, "Now that's a little boy making music with his Papa."

I left all those questions and anxieties out on the sandbar that day and began to see the adoption through Joe's eyes. The picture was clear and simple. He had just missed me and wanted to know me. That's all.

Patricia Dischler is the author of "Because I Loved You," a book on open adoption. "I Missed You" shares one of the most eye-opening moments of Patricia's story as she learned from her son that adults should never assume they know what a teen is thinking – they should simply ask.
Contact Patricia through her website: www.patriciadischler.com.

My Pieces and My Daughter's Pieces

by Mary Elizabeth Hart

My name on my adoption paperwork is Carol King. I am so not a Carol.

I learned my birth name only recently following the death of my mother. I sat and opened the envelope which held my adoption paperwork. I think I expected change to happen in some way as the result of receiving this information. That didn't happen for me. Only the thought that it really was a good thing that I wasn't Carol. I could not for an instant imagine myself as Carol.

For a long time my views on adoption and my own experience felt as if they were set in concrete. I really thought I had it all down. My own status as an adoptee was a purely personal issue. There were no politics of adoption or community of adoption. For me it was about how my family was formed. End of story. Should the issue arise, and occasionally it did, I would express this view clearly. Adoption had no relevance to my life beyond its role in the formation of my family. And flowing from this view came my belief that as an adoptee I alone should have the right to determine what, if any, role my past should play in my future.

And then it all changed. Not overnight. But steadily and relentlessly. My views on most matters related to adoption have flipped and flipped again. My solid, comfortable concrete has disintegrated. I discovered a new place where views and ideas shift. It is a place where I need to remain ever vigilant to how much my own views must change. The truly amazing thing for me has been the ease with which I slipped from the rigid set-in-concrete person that I was to someone who is comfortable with a much broader range of options. It feels much more comfortable in my new spot. I came to the place where I found I could accept different views. I could also accept the changes in my own views, with equanimity. There was a strength I found in this that I did not know I had. And to be honest a sense of peace.

I travelled to Viet Nam in 2001 on the first of two trips to complete the adoption of our youngest daughter. I landed in Ho Chi Minh City. I stepped off the plane into the sounds and smells of two of the most important years of my growing up. My father had been posted as a diplomat to Viet Nam in the late 1960s. I spent my fifteenth and sixteenth years in Viet Nam. As I walked down the stairs from the aircraft to the tarmac I could not hold back tears. I could not help but think of my mother and father and their journey to become parents. I could not stop myself from thinking about the child they almost adopted, the boy born in Vietnam who would have been my brother.

Adoption came into my life a second time – this time using the side door. This time I was to be a mother. This time the journey required that I sit up and take notice. This time it demanded that I reach out to difference and figure out where I stand. I don't think I will ever put the pieces of Carol King together into the whole of me. I am too hard wired to even begin to think in these terms. I now stand on the side lines watching my daughter's journey. Holding up some sign posts. **Holding back tears as I watch my girl taking the pieces of her own puzzle and place them carefully on the table. It is not easy. Oh boy, it is not easy.** Race makes a difference. Our difference as a family means there is no ducking under the radar. And the brutality of some of this experience is sometimes more than I can bear. As my child tells me of the experience of an older child who bluntly, brutally yells out that she, the princess of the biological family, cannot imagine how angry she would be if her mother "threw her away."

My daughter's mosaic will have more pieces than mine. It will include painful pieces that I escaped. But it will, I hope, also include an openness to change and a comfort that escaped me for many years. She will know that she can move and bend with this as she decides where the pieces fit for her. I can see glimpses now. Her comfort with all the pieces of heritage that belong to her–Canadian, Vietnamese, Irish, Scottish, Czech.

Just recently I overheard a conversation between two little girls. They spoke openly of experiences with ignorant and unkind commentary from peers. They agreed between themselves that these folks had no idea what they were talking about. And then they went on to talk about the day when they themselves would form their families through adoption.

On more than one occasion (including with the adoption community) I have been shut down. As if there was something wrong with me because of the views that I personally held on my own adoption. Used to be if you were interested in connecting with your past you were an ungrateful wretch and possibly disturbed. Now if you choose **not** to connect you are repressed and in denial. What few people say loudly enough, in my opinion, is that no one has any business telling anyone how and what to feel.

It is all going to be just fine. Just fine. It is better than it was. There are more people who actually get it. The ignorance is not quite as appalling as it once was. But we still have miles to go. My daughter, however, has something that eluded me for most of my life. A community. A strong, vibrant community. Fine people to hold onto when the going gets tough because a mother's love is not all that one needs.

Mary Elizabeth Hart lives in Toronto with her family. She is an adult adoptee and mother of two girls, one by birth and one through adoption.

Copy this page

(especially if you are borrowing this from a library!)

Using this page, describe who you are. Complete the sentence "I am . . ."

- From your perspective
- From the perspective of your parents
- From the perspective of your best friend
- From the perspective of your teacher

Now that you've done that, what do you think of who you are? What do like about yourself? What would you like to change? How do you "fit" together? There are no right or wrong answers, just a chance to think about who you are.

The Road by Stacy K. Pearson

This piece was created in complete and ultimate commitment to my emotions at the time. It was a free flow of energy, confusion, loneliness, and searching – all related to my journey as an adopted child. In much of the piece you will see smaller elements reminiscent of father and mother figures... clearly the core of my emotions. However, in all of it I found a beauty and a light. Through all of my negative emotions I discovered that I had an inner strength and believed that my road, my inner strength (even if I didn't exactly know where it came from) would see me through. I discovered that I wasn't floundering in emotion. I was a survivor, and I had a path. All I had to do was trust myself and put one foot in front of the other.

Find Stacy's other art on pages 9, 18, 49, 52, and 151.

I Think There Should Be a Law

by Margot Starbuck

I think there should be a law that parents of people who are adopted shouldn't be able to get divorced, or have cancer, or die, or suffer from mental illness, or become addicted, or go to prison. Wouldn't that be a great law?

Rest assured, as soon as someone puts me in charge of the world I'll get right on it. Nobody, whether they're adopted or not, ever wants that hard stuff to happen. I get that. What makes it a little more unwieldy for those of us who are adopted, though, is that the losses we face, after the ones we've already weathered, can lead us to believe something about ourselves that just isn't true.

My dad—technically "adoptive" dad, though of course he was just Daddy to me—left our house when I was five. My adoptive parents divorced when I was six. Looking back now, I understand that the reason my dad left is because he and my mom couldn't be married anymore. That was the adultish reason. At the time, though, all I knew was that he was leaving me. I learned later that the way I interpreted their divorce, thinking that it was all about me, was completely natural. It's just how kids are wired. When that child is adopted, though, it gets a little bit trickier.

As I was growing up I'd also heard the adultish reason I'd been relinquished for adoption. "Your birthparents loved you and wanted the best for you." It's what I most wanted to believe, and so I did. I loved telling people that I was "loved" and "chosen" and "special." Deep in my bones, though, I wasn't buying it. Instead, a naughty little voice constantly hissed, "If you were really worth sticking around for, your birthparents would have kept you. If you were attractive enough, or precious enough, or worthy enough, they couldn't have helped but fallen in love with you and kept you as their own."

Isn't that the most horrible, sinister lie you've ever heard?

What's worse is that the deceptive voice was so very quiet that I never actually heard it with my ears. The lie was just downloaded straight into the marrow of my bones.

This is why, when my Daddy left, all the naughty voice had to whisper was, "See? Told you. See, Margot? You suspected that you might not be worth sticking around for, and you were right. If you were more attractive or more valuable or more worthy, then your dad couldn't have helped but stay around to be with you."

When I was a teenager, no one could tell by looking at me that I'd swallowed that horrible cancerous lie. On the outside I appeared smiley, sparkly, and amazingly well-adjusted. I was active in my church, I was elected to student council, I played for my high school basketball team. No one ever would have guessed that such a diseased belief was rotting inside me.

Looking back now, though, I can see that there had been little clues. For instance, I felt really uncomfortable saying out loud that my friend,

Instead, a naughty little voice constantly hissed:

"If you were really worth sticking around for, your birthparents would have kept you.

If you were attractive enough, or precious enough, or worthy enough, they couldn't have helped but fallen in love with you and kept you as their own."

Isn't that the most horrible, sinister lie you've ever heard?

Mel, was my "best friend." Even though she was. Isn't that weird? Deep down, I didn't believe I was worthy of being someone's best friend. I was afraid that if I said it others would somehow discover what I suspected in my deepest places: that I deserved to be rejected.

I also had more than my fair share of ridiculous—and I do mean ridiculous—"crushes" on boys. It was easier to have a dorky crush than to actually dialogue and risk a real friendship since I didn't believe, deep down, that I was worth knowing.

When I did have a boyfriend my senior year of high school, I naturally assumed we'd break up when I went to college. The day I left for school I was shocked to find out that he hadn't assumed that at all. He thought I was worth caring for even though we were separated by geography. That really blew me away.

I wish I could say that one day, well-loved by him and others, the light bulb just came on and I realized that I was worth being loved. The truth is that the journey toward healing was actually more complicated than that. Part of the reason is that I got a late start. Though some teens wrestle through some hard adoption issues, I didn't give being adopted much thought in adolescence. Because I wouldn't face my feelings, a lot of the junk I'd believed—in my bones—stayed dormant until I was an adult. Sometimes that's what happens. We make it through childhood by using different defenses to protect ourselves. Unfortunately, my defenses failed when I got married. Seriously, it was like someone flipped a crazy switch in my head. When I got married, everything I'd believed about a person—that they were certain to abandon me, since I wasn't worth sticking around for—kind of became activated, like a bad chemical reaction. If that sounds yucky, it was. It totally was. The pain, though, turned out to be the kick in the pants I needed to work toward emotional health.

My journey had a single theme: choosing truth. Rejecting the sinister lies which hissed that I was worthless, I had to choose—again and again—to embrace the truth of who I was. I chose to believe faces, like my husband's, that told me I was acceptable, beloved, precious, worthy. I sought out the eyes and ears and voices of friends and therapists and prayer warriors who reflected for me who I really am. Slowly, truth began to sift down into my marrow. Eventually, I got it—in my bones—that I was worth loving.

Today I'm an adoptive mom. My son is still young. Sometimes, when he spills his drink or loses his sweatshirt or drops his Lego ship, I look at his face and I suspect that he is hearing the same voice I once heard. Though no one else in the room can hear it, I can. Gathering him in my arms, I whisper, "When that just happened, did you hear a voice in your head telling you that you're stupid, that you're worthless?" Brushing away tears, he nods. He knows the sound too well. "I know, baby. I heard it, too, when I was little. But you know what? It just isn't true. That voice is lying. You are not stupid. You are precious and valuable and you are very easy to love. Did you know that? You are easy to love, and I'm so glad you're my son. You are good and I am very very blessed to be your mom."

I want nothing more for him than to receive that truth, deep in his bones.

I have no plans to leave my son. Barring unforeseen circumstances, I don't anticipate that divorce, or illness, or death will take me from him any time soon. Should something outside of my control ever keep me from my son, though, I have one wish for him: to bravely choose the truth of who he is.

I hope it for you, too.

Margot Starbuck, a writer and speaker, is the author of *The Girl in the Orange Dress: Searching for a Father Who Does Not Fail.* Today, in lieu of wearing either a dress or a ball on her head, Margot feels most comfortable in polka-dot shoelaced sneakers, green glasses, and a jazzy nose ring. Learn more at www.MargotStarbuck.com.

What pieces have you "fit" into your life? How did that happen? Who was involved? How did that make you feel?

Inner Soul -

by Chloe Lauryn America Berger

My inner identity has been discovered

As my shadow has traveled to a new place.

My hair is still dark. I am still short.

Yet something has changed, it's different.

A new piece of the thousand piece puzzle - found!

I know who I am by looking above

I am Latina, I am Jewish, I am Mayan

Looking at the stars from the window

Looking at the stars from Antigua

My identity has chased itself in one big universal spin and twirl.

I can be both parts of the day.

I can be the sun or the moon.

I can be a bird or a fish.

I can be Latina and Jewish.

But what I have come to discover

What I have come to realize

Is that in reality I am only one thing

I am unique, I am me.

Chloe Berger, 17, was inspired to write 'Inner Soul' during her first trip back to her birth country, Guatemala. Her passions include raising awareness on diversity, Broadway, writing poetry, swimming, playing the clarinet, and traveling. She thanks her Pop-Pop for his inspiration and encouragement to pursue writing, her angel, Ga, for inspiring her to live, and her family for their constant love and support.

Best Mates on the Bus

by Gina Hall

In the back of the bus, one of a thousand conversations begins....

Ling: Being adopted makes me even more their kid. They had to go to all this huge bother to get me, not just a quick you know what!

Molly: Hadn't thought of it like that. Do you think my Mum and Dad really wanted me? Hey maybe I was an accidental kid?

Ling: Molly, course your Mum and Dad wanted you, I've heard your Mum telling my Mum how they tried and tried to have you. They're crazy about you, same as mine are about me. Remember when we were late home from town, they all went mental, and grounded us for like forever! Parents only do that when they're crazy about you.

Molly: Ling, how is it you're so smart about all this stuff?

Ling: Maybe 'cos I'm mega brilliant, or maybe 'cos Mum and Dad always talk about stuff with me. Like about being adopted, and feelings, and they're always honest.

Molly: My Mum's always honest about stuff too. Well except when she ate my special cake and said it was the dog!

Ling: I could ask you if it was weird living with your birth Mum and Dad.

Molly: But everyone does that, how's that gonna be weird?

Ling: Everyone doesn't do that, there's kids whose parents are divorced, Ray's dad is dead, Annie's mum lives with her new girlfriend, and Suzie and Ellie have the same Mum and different dads. So what's so different about me?

Molly: Guess so, my mum and dad were yelling at each other last night, I could be one of the divorced kids soon.

Ling: You think so?

Molly: No, they always yell, probably means I'm stuck with them both!

Ling: Want some candy?

Molly: Thanks. So your real mum, do your know anything about her?

Ling: My mum is my real mum, it doesn't get much realer than holding my head when I was sick at Christmas, or cuddling me all night 'cos I was freakin' out.

Molly: Well your other mum then.

Ling: We call her my birthmother.
Molly: Right, yeah, so what do you know about her?
Ling: Nothing
Molly: What, nothing at all?
Ling: No, she had me, she put me outside the orphanage, she went away, end of story.
Molly: You want to know about her?
Ling: I dunno, no, well maybe yes a bit.
Molly: Can you find out?
Ling: Mum says we can try and go back where I was found and ask around, see if anyone remembers anything.
Molly: Your mum's cool, with that?
Ling: Yeah, sure, why not?
Molly: But there's your other mum.
Ling: Like I said she's not my mum, she's my birthmother, and she doesn't know me, probably doesn't love me, or even remember. But my mum's like always there for me. I mean we think about my birthmother sometimes, and it might be good to see her, if I ever could, which is, like, never gonna happen.
Molly: So you're cool with that?
Ling: Well I have to be, no point wanting something you can't have.
Molly: Like a million dollars, or diamonds, or a date with Orlando Bloom?!

Molly: Some kids are weird themselves, I mean Alfie still sticks pencils up his nose and thinks he's funny, and Kelly can't go to school if she hasn't painted her toe nails black, and Evie still has a comfort blanket. You're not gonna take any notice of what they say?
Ling: Guess not, but that thing with the pencils is kind of funny, especially when he wiggles his nose and it looks like he's a space alien.
Molly: Hey, do you think I'm weird?
Ling: 'Course, that's why we're such good mates!
Molly: Sleepover tonight?
Ling: You got hot chocolate and marshmallows?
Molly: Well course I have, tonight it is then!

Gina Hall is a full time mum living in the UK. She is also a writer, a farmer, and she is renovating the old farm house that she shares with her husband, three daughters, sister and father. She wrote 'Best Mates on the Bus' to answer some of the interesting, intrusive, funny, silly questions!

I'm sending You Away for a Year to Save Your Life

by Julie Craft

We had tried everything and nothing worked. We were losing our daughter to depression. I felt I had failed Lauren as a mother and that I had failed Doris, her birthmom, as well. Doris had entrusted me with her baby girl 15 years ago and now she was suicidal. Love wasn't enough anymore, we needed help.

Even though we had talented professionals locally, the distractions were too great. Lauren was filling the void in her heart with drugs, sex, and risky behavior. We couldn't break the cycle of sadness, emptiness, and anger. After three hospital admissions, we finally had a diagnosis--Bipolar Disorder. But we didn't have a plan. We also knew that she was struggling greatly with adoption issues.

With all the strength we could muster, we flew as a family to Utah and enrolled her in a therapeutic boarding school. She would have daily group therapy and weekly individual therapy. Her prescribed medication would be monitored by a psychiatrist. Then we went home to grieve.

Only with the help of other parents via parents support groups and seminars, e-mails and phone calls, did we survive the first few months Lauren was there. As we learned more about her needs, we came to understand how adoption had left her feeling very abandoned. Ironically, Sherrie Eldridge's book *Twenty Things Adopted Kids Wish Their Adoptive Parents Knew* came out within a month of her admission. In October. It took me a month to get through the first chapter, then I embraced it.

I took my copy and wrote in the margins, in the corners; I highlighted and underlined. I tried to explain to my daughter where I felt I'd succeeded and where I'd failed. Now I understood why she sabotaged her birthdays, why she felt abandoned–even surrounded by all our love. I sent it to her. It was the turning point.

She wasn't alone. The poems in the book gave her a voice; the pictures gave her a vision. She started doing collages about adoption. First very negative and sad with words like isolated, fantasy, pain, in the dark, and lost. She wrote poems, drew pictures and talked. In the meantime, I was searching for her birthmom. I contacted the liaison that put us together sixteen years ago. He not only still had contact, but Doris had married Lauren's birthfather. We had found them both! I used her poems and stories to form questions for him to answer for us, either on his own or by asking her birthmom. Then I flew to her school and gave her her adoption story, her history, her past, her faith. The relief was obvious. The tears were uncontrollable.

What made me the most proud was seeing Lauren's letters to her birthparents. She wrote them from 1500 miles away. There was no one there to coach her, instruct her, and advise her about what to say or how to say it. These were letters of such importance. And they were amazing. She was kind, loving, grateful, curious, honest, and forgiving. She could balance her own desire for love and attention with a true concern for her birthparent's fears, loss, guilt, and grief. I was never more proud of her than when I forwarded those letters. My daughter wasn't lost. Today she says, "I am what I am and I am who I want to be."

Julie Craft is the Co-Founder and President of The Adoption Support Center, Inc. in Indianapolis, Indiana. Julie is the biological parent of Lindsey and adoptive parent of Lauren. Both daughters involved themselves in work at the agency. Lindsey became an international home study specialist (then later a Pediatric Registered Nurse), while Lauren openly shared her struggles and triumphs as an adoptee and became peer support for birthmothers.

Lauren's Story

by Lauren Hamilton

Fourteen months ago today I was enrolled in a boarding school in Laverkin, Utah. I can't say that I was too fond of that idea and I can't say that I was very happy either. My mom decided to send me to Cross Creek School after years of lying, manipulating, skipping school, doing drugs, overdosing, having sex, etc. I wasn't the "perfect" child parents wish they could raise. I wasn't happy either. My whole life was just going downhill.

I decided to start working the program and no, it was not easy. It was stressful and very sad. There were times when all I wanted was to come back home. I didn't understand even for the longest time why my family, who said they loved me, would want to send their child away. This was when I first felt my abandonment scar. Things of adoption came up for me so bad that I was just depressed to the point where I isolated myself and stopped being motivated. I had a lot of setbacks in the program but one of the things that I learned the most was that I could not give up if it meant the life of me.

I pushed and pushed and pushed myself back up to the top and back on those levels. Being a resident in Utah and living at Cross Creek away from home, I learned to become more and more independent. I wanted to love and respect myself. So, I decided to do some work on me and realize what it is about myself that I like opposed to what is negative. I learned what my dreams and goals were for my life and one dream that came to mind over any other was my dream of meeting my birth family. For a while I dealt with a lot of feelings and long-lost pain. There was a lot there for a 15-year- old.

Back at home, my mom began searching and then with God's help found my birth family. It was without my knowledge at first. My grandpa had met my birthmom's boss at the post office and had been exchanging pictures of me so that my birthmom could see me and know what I was up to for 15 years. It was amazing. I got letters from my mom that were quoted from my birth family and I began to feel closer and closer to them. This was a dream come true for me. I was allowed to have a pass with my mom at home and we got to talking about my birth family and ended up talking to them personally over the telephone. I felt myself being pulled closer to God and realizing that he was really there to help me, knowing that I had a lot of pain, hurt, and emptiness that came from the adoption.

Today I can say that I am successful and that is my success story. I am proud and I always will be. I have respect for myself and confidence that comes from within. If it were not for me choosing to do the things that I did at home that got me sent to the program in Utah, then I can guarantee I would probably not be living here this day. I would like to thank my family, Sherrie Eldridge, me, and most of all God for allowing the things that happened.

Lauren Hamilton was a 16-year old adoptee who compiled the Past, Present, and Future collages on the following page while in counseling at a therapeutic boarding school. After turning her life around, she became an adoptee advocate at The Adoption Support Center in Indianapolis, married, and had a son. She was fatally injured in an auto accident, three months shy of her 21st birthday.

The Collage

Lauren was 1500 miles from home in a therapeutic boarding school when she was ready to examine her feelings. Her therapist assigned her a project, a series of collages; and she chose the topic of adoption. They were rough. Nothing was cut with scissors or perfectly aligned. Pictures were limited and carefully chosen. She scoured through magazines tearing out photos, phrases, headlines and pictures that spoke to her. What she found was spooky.

These were much more than words she would have chosen, more than words she had chosen in the past to explain her feelings about adoption. She created three collages that represented her PAST, PRESENT and FUTURE. In the PAST collage, "sophomore slump" represented the year in school when she crashed, her first suicide attempt. "Jones" was her birthmother's name and ironically slang for drugs. "Lost in Space" and "Children need help to develop" were phrases that cleverly described her feelings. Her PRESENT collage included words and phrases of advice and inspiration. "It's your life - fill it up", "Take comfort", and "The chemistry's just beginning" – these spoke of the transition she was feeling as she absorbed new information about her birth family. Her page on the FUTURE was totally upbeat – "A dream come true", "Being me", and "The greatest experience of my life" showed her optimism and excitement. And imagine finding this phrase, "The day seemed magical. They opened up their hearts to each other. They confided intimacies, confident of each other's acceptance." These are the words that spoke to her, for her. The collages were a way of finding the words she couldn't find.

Try making your own collages.

Go through magazines and newspapers looking for words, images, and pictures that represent your Past, Present, and Future. Then, get some scissors and glue and create them! Don't be in a hurry. Take some time. When you're done, look at them. What do they tell you about your pieces and how they fit together in your life? Share with someone if you feel comfortable doing so.

Sharing the Pieces

The great thing about puzzles is that when they are completed, you want to show them off. You want others to see and share with you your wonderful accomplishment.

It is the same with our lives as adoptees. When we find a piece that fits, we want to share it, and we want others to experience who we are and the excitement we felt when we figured it out!

That is what this section is about – how adoptees share the pieces of who they are. In here you will find inspirational messages and messages of hope. You will find poems and stories of adoptees who seek understanding from others. And you will find burdens and struggles, because sometimes the world out there is not too friendly to the "me" inside each of us.

But we still share, and that is what these people do. Find out what they share, how they share it, be inspired, and feel connected. Recognize that sharing is not always met with open arms, but that our desire for others to see us as we are never fades away.

I just want to fit in
Just want to be like a normal family
I wish I could pick out my own clothes
I want to invite friends over and go to friends' houses
I would like to attend after school activities
I want to feel love when I walk in the door
I need someone to take on the adult responsibilities
I just want to be like a normal kid
I hope to be a good parent some day
I never want to leave my kids
Will someone listen to me?
Let me decide
I want some closure
I'm tired of taking care of my siblings
Who will come to my band concert?
THIS IS JUST BETWEEN US
I can't remember what my dad looks like
Why didn*t my parents come to see me?
Is my dad still in jail?
Can I see my brother?
IS MY MOM STILL TAKING DRUGS?
When will we go to court?
What did the judge say?
Where will I live?
What if I don't like it there?
Can my sisters come?
Do they really want me?
Will they send me back?
Don't tell anyone about this.
Why did my parents leave me?
ARE THEY COMING BACK?
Will I ever see them again?
Did I do something wrong?

The author is an advocate for abused and neglected children in the foster care system. Her submission represents the voices of children experiencing the pain of being separated from their families.

who am i ?

By Jonathan Riley

I might not be exactly who you think I am. Living not knowing who my real parents are feels like a leech, keeping the very thought of comfort away, latching onto every vulnerability in my mind, and popping up in the worst possible moments. This is the life I live. It feels like I'm in the middle of nowhere searching for people that I don't even know, much less what their names are. I feel concealed and unknown behind a blurred tapestry, unable to share my thoughts with others. When I open myself up to people, I get the feeling that if I tell them something, they might tell others what I said in a less accurate way and make my thoughts appear negative. This makes me fearful of what I say to others, even my friends.

There are many things in life that I can't change, such as the way I look. I was born in the Philippines, which is a cluster of islands off the coast of China but still is considered a country, and I was adopted. I may look different from others and often feel that is the way they judge me. Some people look deep inside me and make friends with the real me. But others mistake my appearance and tease me in every possible way. Sometimes people try to get to know me and when they know me too much, they try to get inside me, exposing weaknesses I have, and the worst possible insult that ever was given to me was about me not fitting into my family.

One thing that differentiates me from other people is my unique talents; I'm a singer with massive amounts of expression. I'm fairly agile and strong which, in my case, categorizes me as a gymnast. I have a talent that I don't usually let the world recognize: an ear for music. If you tell me the name of a song you know from a famous movie like Star Wars, give me a day or two and I can play most of the piano music for it, without the sheet music. I possess my own distinctive talents that help me project to the world. But some people don't accept me for who I am.

Even though I don't know my real parents, I know one thing, I am really lucky to have a family such as the one I have now. They are the most caring family I could ever ask for in a million and six years. My mom cares for me when I'm sick, takes me to gym and school every day, helps me when I need assistance and is trustworthy and lovable. My dad is awesome. He lets me play video games, go to movies with him, and is a great guy. My sister is another unique person that is of great importance in my life. She has a disease called Tuberous Sclerosis and it affects her learning, growth and emotions. She had 21 tubers in different parts in her brain. She had seizures every night and even some during the day. Recently, she had brain surgery and they removed 2 tubers from her brain which were causing the seizures. Thankfully it went well and she is doing great. I was praying for her all the way.

I am glad because I have friends and family that care for me and help me when times are rough and things go wrong. I put my faith and trust into each and every one of them and thank God for giving me a great life and I will enjoy it while it lasts.

Jonathan Riley is a 14-year adoptee from the Philippines who currently resides in the state of Colorado. His work entitled, "Who Am I?" expresses what it means to feel different and needing to make unnecessary changes in order to fit in. An avid reader and a lover of music, he does his best to be himself, and eventually hopes to become a famous musician.

IS IT ME OR MY MASK?

by Angel Coldiron, LPC

I don't really know. For such a long time, they were one and the same—or at least I thought so. This mask was made of steel and impenetrable. This mask would stop any outside hurt from coming in and any emotions of mine from coming out. This mask was smiling ALL of the time, but the mouth behind it could barely form a grin most of the time. Tears would fall from my eyes, but they would fall behind the mask and land in the crevices of my heart. This mask attracted the popular crowd because it made me seem like I had the perfect life—because remember, I was smiling all of the time. This mask actually made me think I had the perfect life because when I looked in the mirror, the mask wouldn't let me see the real me. This mask is what kept any thoughts or emotions about my birth family tucked deep inside of me. This mask silenced questions that I had about my adoption. Because I have worn the mask most of my life, I thought it was a true part of me.

While I have learned that yes, it is a part of me, it no longer defines me. I am now learning who I truly am without the mask. It's been difficult because it's hard to take something off that has been cemented on for over 20 years. It was painful to pull off, and many times, the harder I worked to pull it off and see what was behind it, the harder it resisted. I realized I was pulling too hard. If I just took one piece of the mask off at a time, I wasn't as fearful to see what was actually behind it.

I wish that as a teenager I would have had the courage to take my mask off so I could work toward being genuinely happy much earlier in my life. My mask protected me from everything—or so I thought. However, it wasn't protecting me from myself, and as the saying goes, sometimes you can be your own worst enemy. True healing comes when the mask is taken off slowly. Healing leads to forgiveness, happiness, and peace. Sometimes, when things get tough, I get out my mask and put it on, but I am in control of the mask now rather than it being in control of me.

Angel Coldiron is 27 years old and is from Jefferson , NC . She is a former foster child who was adopted when she was 1 ½ years old. She currently works with foster families and is a Licensed Professional Counselor. Her writings reflect her journey as an adoptee as well as the struggles of other foster children and adoptees she has met along the way.

A Use for Your Senses
By Sheila Black

Your eyes are for seeing,
Seeing the longing in my heart.

Your mouth is for speaking,
To comfort me when things are dark.

Your nose is for smelling
The sweet love that I have.

Your hands are to hold me
Whenever things are bad.

Your ears are for listening.
Listen to my story.
I am an adopted child,
For love I do not worry.

See Sheila's other writing on pages 120 and 125.

Just a Thought
Chris Abbott

Think it's important to
Support a stumbling arm
Even if only for a tiny stone
For it might be some one's lifetime past
Like a plane appearing from a blanket cloud
Could be running empty, hungry scared
From aborted landing years ago

Chris Abbott is fifty eight years old, an adoptee from London. At the moment she carries a stitched up bag. It holds loads of bits, pieces, and jumbled messages. Many have their roots from her teenage years. Another poem by Chris can be found on page 44.

To tell or not to tell?: A narrative burden

By Bert Ballard

Most of us are probably familiar with Shakespeare's line, "To be or not to be? That is the question." For adoptees though, the question is, "To tell or not to tell?" Many times throughout our lives, someone has discovered we're adopted and that person wants to know more about our story. In that moment, we're faced with a choice: To tell or not to tell our story about how and why we were adopted. It goes something like, "Wow. You're adopted. What's that like?" Or "Tell me your story." Or, "Wow, you're so lucky." And there's a silence afterwards. In that silence, the other person wants you to spill your guts.

I'm here to tell you, you're not alone. Even adult adoptees deal with this. An adult adoptee from Australia told me that she doesn't like to draw attention to herself so she doesn't usually tell that she's adopted. In fact, when she tells others about being adopted the conversation becomes about her and she's not comfortable with that. Another adoptee says the most difficult thing about being an adoptee is repeatedly telling/explaining that he's adopted. The choice to tell or not to tell is a difficult one we struggle with all of our lives.

> To tell or not to tell...That is the question...

I call this choice of "To tell or not to tell?" a narrative burden. Let me explain. A narrative is another term for a story. Everyone has a story about his or her life. When we talk about where we were born or whether or not we like school or what we had for dinner last night, we are telling a story about ourselves. Of course, as adoptees, we have a unique story. Some of us don't know when we were born or what our parents looked like or what time we were born. And some of us might remember our orphanages, foster families, have some memories of our birth parents, or recall meeting our adoptive parents for the first time. Regardless of the exact details, as adoptees we have unique stories others like to hear.

A burden is something that weighs you down. It is something we have to carry. As adoptees, our stories are burdens. They are burdens because of the unique nature of our stories. Because our stories are different than the stories of people who know when they were born or know what their parents look like or know exactly where they were born or know their birth parents, people want to hear our stories. So, we become faced with the question of do we tell others our stories or do we not?

Narrative burden, therefore, means that as an adoptee, you carry around a weight, a burden, a choice to tell your story or to not tell your story. It means that when people ask us to tell our story we have a choice to make because of the nature of our story. Generally, biological children don't have this. Nobody asks them to tell their story. Only adoptees it seems face this constant question, this burden. And especially if your skin color is different than others around you, people are more likely to ask about your story.

So, how do you deal with this narrative burden? Is there anything that can be done about it? There may be times when you wish you were not asked. Or there may be times when you don't want to have to decide . . . again. Or you may wish there was a way to tell the story without having to say anything.

As an adoptee, I'd like to say, yes, there's a simple clear cut answer or easy way to deal with the narrative burden. I'd like to give you a magic pill. But the fact of the matter is that there isn't one. The narrative burden is something that is a part of who we are.

While I can't give you a magic pill, I can offer you some advice, some thoughts that can help you figure out how to deal with your narrative burden, with the question of "To tell or not to tell?"

The first piece of advice I have is that your narrative burden is an indicator of your uniqueness. Sometimes it isn't any fun to be asked, but people ask because they are curious or find something interesting about you. And, you know what, that is a good thing! It means you're unique, you're different, and you're unlike anybody else. I encourage you to be proud of who you are and to be proud of your unique story. See each opportunity of wondering to tell or not to tell as a chance to talk about yourself and to share your story in a fun way. Your narrative burden does not have to be a burden, but can point toward how unique, different, and interesting you are!

The second piece of advice I have is to see your narrative burden as an opportunity to get to know someone else. Some of us don't like talking about ourselves, so we can always share just a bit and then ask them about their story. As an adoptee, I was always intrigued by others' stories. "You mean you know what time you were born? Your parents can tell you what happened?" Sure, I was jealous, but I also got to know the other person better and develop a friendship with them. When we share and ask others, we find we are both sharing and it doesn't feel as heavy a burden. This way, I'm no longer in the spotlight, but I'm sharing my story and hearing others'. I've chosen to tell, but it doesn't feel like quite a burden. Not only am I redirecting the conversation, but now I'm also developing a friendship with and learning about someone else.

The third piece of advice is probably the most important. **Never forget that your story is and always will be yours!** Your story, your narrative is yours – no one else's! And you don't have to share it if you don't want to. And you can share as much as you want to! The choice is yours, and your burden isn't necessarily a bad thing, but also a beautiful thing.

This Is My Life
Song by Bec, Jodie, Ally & Kerry-Ann, adoptees who live in Australia

Got a story to tell
That I need you to know
There is no shame
Close your eyes and listen to what I have to say

I'm a dandelion
That's been blown away
To start a new life
To start a new day

Chorus
This is my life
Not a fairy tale but it's reality
This is my life
Though the seasons keep changing I will still be me
And I'm holding on 'cause
This is my life

Everything seemed to be closing in around
Til you came and set me free
Love found me in a moment of truth
Now there's no doubt
I'm where I'm supposed to be

Chorus
This is my life
Not a fairy tale but it's reality
This is my life
Though the seasons keep changing I will still be me
And I'm holding on 'cause
This is my life

In 2006, the Post Adoption Resource Centre in Sydney, Australia worked with eight teenage adoptees to make a film about being adopted. The group, who were all girls, met regularly over about six months to work on the film, and became good friends as they shared their stories about being adopted. The girls wrote and recorded to two songs to use in the film – "Just Like You" (see page 129) and "This is my Life". The film was launched late in 2006, and is called "The Girl in the Mirror".

Your story is an amazing thing. And it is something to be valued. It is something you can choose to share or not to share . . . or to share some parts and not others. Your story is a unique thing, and it is a privilege to have. But that does not mean it always has to be shared. The choice to tell or not to tell is yours because it is your story and no one –not even your birth parents or your adoptive parents – can choose to tell it. They have their stories and they can choose to tell them, but you have your own story that is all yours. What an amazing gift!

Of course, if you choose not to share, don't be rude. You can politely decline. You can say, "I don't want to talk about that right now, but what about you?" or "I'm not comfortable talking about that right now." You can value and treasure your story by keeping it sacred and special without telling it to anyone. Or you can value and treasure it by telling your story in all its drama. Or, you can tell a little bit sometimes and more at other times. **The choice is yours, and that is a good thing!**

Here's a final piece of advice. More of a secret actually. The narrative burden never goes away. For example, just a week ago I met with a group of friends who knew I was from Vietnam, but didn't know I was adopted. They asked when I came out of Vietnam or if I knew my parents. I responded, "Three weeks and no." Well, obviously it was clear that I was adopted and immediately came the silent pause, the unspoken, "Tell us more about it! We want to know." And then I had a choice, To tell or not to tell?

I would like to say that the narrative burden goes away, but it doesn't. But, if you learn now how to deal with it, it gets a little bit easier. You also learn to accept that burden and see it not as a difficult choice, but as a celebration of who you are as a unique person. You learn to tell more to some and not to others. You learn to enjoy the attention at times and at other times see it as a chance to get to know others and share.

The choice never goes away, but you learn to accept it and yourself. For me? Well, in this case, I told a little bit and then asked about everyone else. I wasn't ready at that time to tell my whole story. Maybe next time I will be. But you know what? That's okay. Because in the end, it's my story, and I'm proud of it, even if I don't always share it all the time.

Remember that the narrative is yours, all yours. And the burden – well, that just goes along with being adopted. It's part of what it means to be uniquely us. We don't always like it. But maybe when we're faced with the question of to tell or not to tell we can remember that it's because we are unique and different and interesting. And hopefully if we remember that, it won't be as much of a burden as it is a celebration.

Bert Ballard is a Vietnamese adoptee and editor of this book. You can read more about him in the introduction. In addition to all of that stuff in there, he really likes Asian food, is married (look for Sarah Ballard in this book), has two girls and is awaiting a referral for a son from Vietnam. In his spare time he is a professor of communication at the University of Waterloo in Ontario, Canada.

This song is for my parents and for adoptive parents everywhere.

Somewhere in the Middle

By Jared Rehberg (find him on Facebook)

If you could only see the world through my eyes. D Bm G A
Carry all the weight of one race, in my disguise. D Bm G A
There's nothing to say to heal the pain. Em A
I'm reminded that I'm different, every time I say my name. A G A

chorus:
I'm somewhere in the middle, somewhere in between. D A G A
and I hope I made you proud for just being me. D G G A
I can't change my past or who I'm supposed to be. Bm Bm G A
I'm adopted by destiny and loved by you. D A G D

Tell me about your life and the struggles you went through. D Bm G A
Maybe we'll find common ground, let's talk about you. D Bm G A
You gave me the tools, to follow all my dreams Em A
and I know it wasn't easy, somehow we made it through. A G A

chorus:
I'm somewhere in the middle, somewhere in between. D A G A
And I hope I made you proud for just being me. D G G A
I can't change my past or who I'm supposed to be. Bm Bm G A
I'm adopted by destiny and loved by you. D A G D

There will be people who stop and stare. D Bm G A
They won't understand us and the bond we share. D Bm G A
You might have to speak up to help them understand Em A
And I will love you the best that I can. A G A

chorus:
I'm somewhere in the middle, somewhere in between. D A G A
and I hope I made you proud for just being me. D G G A
I can't change my past or who I'm supposed to be. Bm Bm G A
I'm adopted by destiny and loved by you. D A G D

Jared Rehberg is a 34-year old Vietnamese adoptee from Northboro, MA. "Somewhere in the Middle" is a dedication to his amazing parents, Rick and Rita Rehberg. Jared currently lives in Queens, NY with his wife, Ying. For more information visit www.jaredrehberg.com

Three Wishes

By Sheila Black

If I could have three wishes
What would they be?
The first of the three
Would definitely be:
Even though we're different,
at peace we would be.

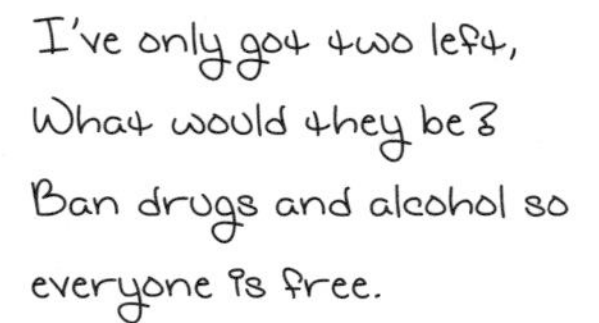

I've only got two left,
What would they be?
Ban drugs and alcohol so
everyone is free.

Also, give every foster child
a great adoptive home
Just like me.

The author, Shelia Black, is 12 years old. She is waiting for her adoption to be finalized. Find Sheila's other poems on page 115 and 125

If you had one wish, but could only use it to change the world in some way, what would you wish for?

Grounding

by Kathy Mason

When things fall apart
and moorings come loose

Think of yourself as a safety caboose

Riding behind a life long train

That travels the earth and sky domain

Plant your feet deep in the earth

And know this as your place of birth

Reach your arms up to the sky

Never forget that you can fly.

Remember please who you truly are

A bright and shiny, lovely star.

Kathy Mason is a social worker who lives in North Carolina with her husband and two German Shepards. She has two grown sons.

Advice from a teen adoptee

By Katya Dato Chancellor

Realize adoption is a positive thing because you are chosen. When I found out that I was adopted and every time someone has left my life, it was always really hard on me and I felt unwanted. For the longest time I didn't think being adopted was a good thing. But I've come to realize I was chosen to be a part of a family and that is a really good thing.

Be proud to be adopted I always find it funny when people say "Oh you look just like your mother." It's great to tell them that we are not blood related and that I am adopted. And of course they always say from where? And when I tell them Russia they are really surprised and they always want to know my story, so it is great to be able to have a unique family story. Every other person I know who is adopted has their own story. Be proud, tell it.

Accept that you're your own person and not be forced to fit into a mold. My family and I are completely different. While they wouldn't socialize much with neighbors, I would. My mother calls me a social butterfly and I couldn't be contained. I was that little girl who knew my neighbors and knew who had pets and their names. I would hang out with my neighbors instead of my friends my own age. Almost anywhere I go I would make a new friend.

Be open to different views and ideas, don't put them down. Accept yourself but still work on improving and changing yourself to become a better person. And sometimes that means considering ideas that you originally thought were stupid.

Embrace your similarities, but acknowledge your differences. Even though I am very different from my family, and we don't always agree with one another, being different is

Owing

Kim Eun Mi Young

I owe you nothing
I give to you
Love
Fidelity
Trust

You owe me nothing
You give to me
Family
Belonging
Connectedness

Owing brings forth
resentment
debt
and when it's paid
it's final

Giving offers
warmth
love
joy
it is always held close
to the heart

Find other poetry by Eun Mi on pages 43, 53, 60, 73, and 148.

battle cry/undone

by juli jeong martin

white feminine standards
of beauty and place
declare deviance
like it was going out of style
putting value on face, and
value on space
empty callow bodies shallow
i was that girl on the exam table
desiccated body devastated soul.

indoctrinated at thirteen
i've been running ever since
but it's every channel, every screen
every glossy magazine
blares "this is what woman looks like"
that i should lengthen my legs
with vertical stripes
and always dress for my
body type.

well, i've got news for you, world
i like my breasts bound
i'll wear my hair buzzed despite
my face being round
and my legs are just fine
in low slung men's jeans
defying your norms
of what my body means.

defying your norms
with my figure my form
one more in the swarm
of gender offenders
i aggravate, deviate
stand up and agitate
and as much as you denigrate
this thing i become
you cannot silence
i won't be undone.

you cannot silence
we won't be undone.

Find more of Juli's thoughts on pages 28, 47, 72, and 142.

good because you get exposed to things that you might not have ever thought you would like. It is good to find out things you don't like that you stay away from. You also realize that people who are different can still be good people and can also help you with the things you don't do well.

Find the trust in your family. The more I spend time with my family, I get closer and trust them more each day, even thought I don't agree with everything they want and say. I was lied to in the beginning of my relationship with my family, and it was rocky at first. After I found out my family was not responsible for the lie, it makes me trust them more. Ever since, I have been working on trust. But nobody is perfect and people make mistakes. Forgiveness is important.

Spend quality one on one time with each person in your family. It really helps to get to know everyone in your family on a personal level, with doing something new or something that you both enjoy. My dad would take me on business trips once a year to places that had something that I would really like. One year he took me to Denver, Colorado with him. We stayed on a ranch that had horses, goats, and dogs that we saw every morning in front of our window. I got to ride the biggest horse even though I was the smallest guest there. It doesn't have to be anything big and fancy.

No time limit to bond If you put any limits on anything you might be disappointed. Some things just take more time but it is important to work at bonding and not give up. There are so many different ways to bond.

Finding a common bond It took me until freshmen year of high school to really bond with my mother. She would always tell me that she was on my side, but I never really understand what she meant. I finally figured out how much she does for me and sacrifices for me. She cares more about my happiness and making my life a success. When I was younger and we would fight I would bring out the "You're not my real mother" card. I knew it would hurt her, but didn't care at the time. I was just wanted to win the argument. But now it doesn't come across that she's not my "real mother" but then again what counts as a real mother? It's someone that is there for you, cares for you, and loves you unconditionally, and you feel the same way.

Find adoptee support groups (I know it sounds cheesy) I'm not one to really go to support groups but I went to one and got things off my chest. I know that you can't express your feelings, frustrations, and thoughts out to anyone but other adoptees and because they really understand what you're going through. They have gone through it, too.

Learn from everyone – Sibling, friends, and others (family members) all have something to teach. Look for the good in everybody in your family, even your siblings. My brother and I are very close in age (nine months and eight days apart) with him being older. We get along, but fight just like siblings do. That's never going to change. We have the same sense of humor and that's what we really bond over; something small can make us close. A lot of older brothers that I know are very protective of their little sisters, but my brother doesn't really show it. He cares, he just has a funny way of showing it.

Don't resent your birth parents It's a lot easier to say you hate your birth parents and hate that they left you, but that's not going to make anything better. It's not going to make you feel good to hate someone you hardly know or someone who's not in your life any more. You shouldn't worry always about other people. Be a little selfish and worry about you.

Even though my family and I don't have a lot of similarities, the similarities that we do have make us closer and make us a family. Like every family there are fights, arguments, and words that are said out of anger but I would not change it for anything.

Katya Dato Chancellor is 20 years old and she lives in Pittsburgh, PA. She is originally from Russia. Her two passions are art and animals, and she has found a way to combine both into one (www.katyaspet.blogspot.com). This is one of the first pieces of art she did of a favorite foster, Eddie Bonz. He was found cold, emaciated, and homeless. Without volunteers, staff, and his will to live he would not be with a loving family today.

Giving Back to My Homeland

by Kahleah Maria De Lourdes Guibault

My name is Kahleah Maria De Lourdes Guibault, and I am seventeen years old. I was born in Malacatan, Guatemala on February 28th, 1991. I was relinquished at birth for adoption by my birthmother due to extreme poverty. My first mothers' dreams were that I would "be adopted, receive medical care, be fed, clothed and educated." I lived in my birth-country for just five months in a foster family before being adopted by my loving family in Canada on August 2nd, 1991.

Guatemala is one of the smallest countries in Central America and with a population of 12.7 million, it is the most populated. Even more surprising is the fact that approximately sixty percent of the country is currently living below the poverty line. This has caused Guatemala's infant mortality rate to be one of the highest in all of Central and South America: forty one percent. Along with a high infant mortality rate and a low life expectancy, most Guatemalans face the problems of illiteracy, corruption, malnutrition, and severely unjust wages.

My numerous humanitarian trips back to my country of birth have shown me just how lucky I am. Had I survived and not been adopted, I would most likely be living an impoverished life just like the majority of my fellow Guatemalans. I most certainly would not have had the opportunity to have an education. Education means so much to me. I have taken it upon myself to better the lives of as many children in Guatemala as I possibly can. My future goals include starting my own non-profit, charitable and humanitarian organization in Guatemala to help the children who need and deserve aid.

I have already started to change the lives of many in Guatemala by raising money over the last eight years and plan to keep doing so as I pursue future projects. The passion I have for humanitarian work is immense. I feel this comes from my innate sense of where I came from. I also know where I belong and where I am going. I truly believe that one person can indeed change the world...even if it is simply helping one child at a time.

Kahleah is an 18 year old adoptee from Guatemala. She has enjoyed a close relationship with her beloved foster family in Guatemala. Kahleah also experienced a reunion with her brother's Colombian birth family. Kahleah has shared her thoughts on adoption with numerous adoption publications including PACT, Adoption Today and Adoptive Families Magazine. Kahleah lives with her family in Halifax, Nova Scotia and will be starting university in the fall.

Legacy

by Sheila Black

A wise figure told me once
That in this journey we call life,
No one is more important than another,
No less is each one's strife.
Sometimes the brightest stars that shine
Are not the ones we've named,
It matters not the size of them
But who burns the brightest flame.
If you toss a stone into the water
Of a still and peaceful lake,
Watch close the outward ripples
As they spread their ceaseless quakes.
In life we are the stars, the stones,
  the hero, and the sinner,
But how we learn from each event
Defines the losers and the winners.
Leave behind a caring legacy
With each person that you meet.
And they will prove that with compassion
Life can be complete.

Find Sheila's other poems on page 115 and 120.

No More Running: Moving Beyond Foster Care

By Sarah Callihan

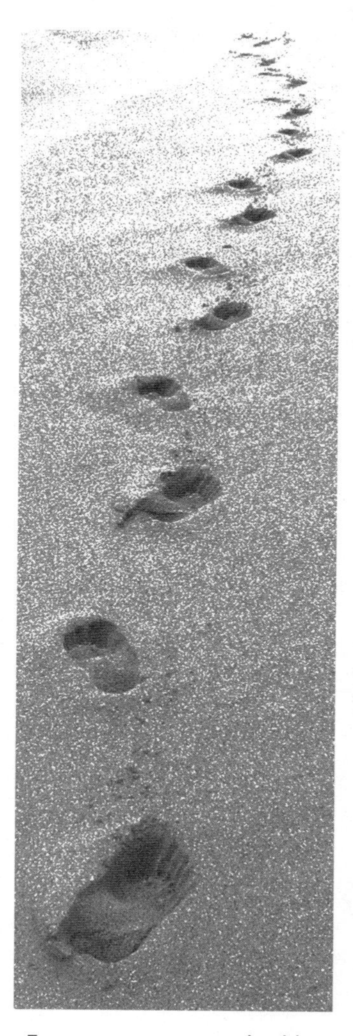

Hi! My name is Sarah and I wanted to tell you a little bit about my experiences in the system. I was in the foster care system for 6 years all at the same placement. I was placed there with my younger brother when I was almost 12 and stayed until I was 18 and went off to college. My childhood was not a childhood at all in my eyes. I was abused every way you could think of–emotionally, mentally and physically. My mom was sick and so I had to grow up really fast because my sister was not willing to step up to the plate as the oldest. All of this changed when I was taken away from my family and placed in the middle of nowhere with strangers. Imagine being a 12 year old city girl and being plucked from everything you have ever known and placed in the country where you only have one neighbor. That would be me. Right off the bat, I was diagnosed with depression and sent to counseling. That at least helped me through the trial that I went through against my dad for the abuse I endured.

Living in foster care was a culture shock for me because everybody was so different from what I was used to. The biggest change was that my foster mom is Jewish. I was brought up "Christian" but I didn't know what I necessarily believed. I dealt with all my changes the same way that I did as a child, I threw myself into schoolwork and extras. When I was at home, I was in my room with my nose in a book or outside playing basketball.

I was doing well in that placement, after giving myself an attitude adjustment, when I hit a snag. My mom, who had been battling multiple sclerosis for 9 years, by now had passed away. I never got to say goodbye. I became deeply depressed and questioned God. Nobody noticed except for a good friend. I always had a 'happy go lucky sarcastic' mask on. A year later, my senior year of high school, my grandfather passed away from cancer that he didn't tell anyone had come back. I pushed myself harder and graduated from high school. I was also admitted into college, the first person in my family to do so. I was ecstatic.

For so many years I had been told that I would never amount to anything and would end up like my mom. My mom was a teenage mother who by the time she was 26 had three children, a marriage that was starting to become unhappy and a high school education. **I was told two extremes growing up: I would end up barefoot and pregnant and drop out of high school or that no man would ever want to be with me and I would still amount to nothing. I overcame these both when I was admitted into college.**

When I started college, I was in the Independent Living program through my county and dealt with another culture shock. I had never been around so many international people my age before and it made me curious. I was an education major at that time and wanted nothing more than to finish school and become a high school history teacher in a small town. I soon discovered where my passions lie: helping people. I decided to stick it out with education and find somehow to do advocacy or something on the side. However, after 4 years of struggling and not being happy, I changed my major. I changed to criminal justice with a minor in political science. I also realized that what I want to do the most was to work with battered women and abused and neglected children and teenagers. If I could incorporate that into my major everything would be great. I also was put in touch with Ohio's Foster Care Alumni Association's communications chair, Lisa. She helped me put my voice out there.

For years I had been journaling and blogging to help me deal with all the changes, ups and downs in my life and never really shared them with anyone who understood. I had felt like I was alone my entire life that nobody understood but me, which was how I viewed trust as well. I never really 100% trusted anyone, not even my family. However when I met Lisa and she told me about what was going on with the public funds that support foster care, I thought "here is my chance to make a difference in someone's life." So, I testified before the Ohio House of Representatives to argue for why those funds should continue. The giving of these funds would not have mattered to me since I was already 23 almost 24 and had been out of the independent living program for a couple of years. I thought that maybe if just one person could get help to go to school and to make their life better with my help that would make all the difference for my own life.

I got through my childhood, adolescence and am now in my young adulthood. I don't know how I survived it all, just by sheer luck and the grace of God I suppose. I am still there for my family–all 4 of them. I have made friends with people from all over the world because I took a chance at going to college instead of letting the people from my past have what they wanted: for me to fail. I am now going into graduate school in the hopes of one day becoming a Criminal Justice professor. I am also looking into maybe one day becoming a CASA (Court Appointed Special Advocate) worker and a foster/adoptive parent once I have a stable income and place to live. **I don't really see myself as a role model or anything important. I am just someone who had a horrendous childhood, an all right adolescence and am striving to have a good life as an adult. I am a normal person; I just overcame many obstacles to get to where I am.**

Sarah Callihan is a 24 year old former foster child from Dayton, OH. Her story, "No More Running: Moving Beyond Foster Care," came out of wanting to help other children and teens that might be going through the same or similar life issues. She is dealing with issues but hopes to become a college professor and foster parent in the future.

What do you wish others knew about you? Why?

DNA SONG

Lyrics by Alison Larkin

As an adopted kid I didn't know about my kin.
When I looked into the mirror I was always wondering
If the face before me looked like anyone at all
I loved my folks, but I wanted to know, would I be
short or tall?

And then I found the truth about my past.
When I found my birth parents at last.
The truth isn't always easy, but it was mine to know,
And freed me up to be myself at last.

They say the truth will set you free
That certainly was true for me
Hear the words I have to say
In this wee song of mine today

To solve your inner mystery
It helps to know your history
Every child born today
Deserves to know their DNA.

They say the genes count for a lot,
and I'm not meaning Levi's
From can you curl your tongue?
To can you roll your eyes?
To will you be a diabetic? Will you have a stroke?
When medicine can save a life it stops being a joke.

Even President Obama had to go and find his father,
He knows what it's like to need to know.
It's hard to be a future star
if you do not know who you are,
Every child should have the right to know.

They say the truth will set you free
That certainly was true for me
Hear the words I have to say
In this wee song of mine today

To solve your inner mystery
It helps to know your history
Every child born today
Deserves to know their DNA.

From Alison...

While every human being should have the right to know the facts about their family history, sometimes, for whatever reason, they just can't. I believe that we are always connected to our birth family, whether or not we meet them. I believe our personalities, interests and deepest instincts are passed on to us, through the genes, from our birth parents and their parents before them, going way, way back.

Even if our adoptive family is very different from us – although I love my parents dearly, mine are very different from me – I believe that if we can get still and trust what the adopted heroine of "The English American" calls her 'knower' – well, that's our deepest self guiding us. It's our DNA talking. It is, perhaps, the spirit of our ancestors helping us figure out who we really are, so we can choose what works for us, discard what doesn't and set about creating a life that we truly love.

Alison Larkin is a comedienne, adopted person and bestselling author of "The English American, a novel."

To hear Alison singing this song go to www.alisonlarkin.com

Just Like You

by Adopted Teens

Chorus
I breathe just like you
I love just like you
I breathe just like you
I feel just like you

Verse One
Sometimes I think what I could be,
In another life, in another world.
Would I be safe?
Would I be free?
Would I be anything like me?

Chorus
I breathe just like you
I love just like you
I breathe just like you
I feel just like you

Verse Two
I have someone who cares for me
The others here are family
The living's in the here and now
This family tree has another bough

There is a place that I will call my own
I won't be left again
I'll always have my home

Chorus x 2
I breathe just like you
I love just like you
I breathe just like you
I feel just like you

Teen adoptees from Australia who worked with the Post Adoption Resource Centre in Sydney on the song above and information for the film "The Girl in the Mirror." See another song on page 117.

An Innocent Grows Up

by Xiu Xiu Coone

A young hungry toddler
Looking for a family,
wishing to be wanted
Adopted at last
On my first day of school
cried for my new mom
To comfort me,
wanted only her love

An innocent long ago
I find myself
not such an innocent now
Almost grown up
I will never forget
nor will I ever regret
The loneliness of my early youth

I go to reconnect in my homeland
And meet kids in an orphanage
Innocent
I learn about the strife
of my heritage
Now comes the time
I can make a difference

17-year old Xiu Xiu (Ai Xiu Angeleigh Pilialoha Cooney) is from Nanjing, China and spent most of her childhood in Kobe, Japan. Now she lives, laughs, and loves in Honolulu and has become a "local girl" on the islands. She dedicates her life to helping others while she explores the beauty and wonders in this world. See Xiu Xiu's other writing on page 152.

Coming Out Again

by Patrick McMahon

Outside, morning air is cool and crisp, but the October sun is promising to create Indian summer. I sit at my desk and begin the letter, the one put off so many times in the four months since I turned my world upside down with that first phone call. Dear Barb? Dear Mom? Three newsy, rambling paragraphs flow out on to the page. The weather. Working as a courier driver. Going to photography exhibits.

Okay. Enough chitchat. I get up, go out on the deck, feel the warm sun on my face, affirm that I want this new relationship with my birthmother to be based on honesty, take many deep breaths, return to the desk, and take the plunge.

Among the many other things I want to tell you about me, one is that I'm gay. It's important to me that you know that because it's something I've had to come to terms with and now feel someone who knows me must know. I don't make my orientation the center of my life. It is simply a part of who I am. I'll say no more now because I don't know your perceptions of, exposure to, or attitudes toward gay people.

AMONG THE MANY OTHER THINGS I WANT TO TELL YOU ABOUT ME, ONE IS THAT I'M GAY.

I put down the pen and read this paragraph over a couple of times. Yes, that's fine. Short. To the point. I lean back and stare out the window, through the reddish gold maple leaves, trying to get a handle on why my stomach has taken up gymnastics again.

For crying out loud, I'm a gay man who has lived as such for a dozen years. I've demonstrated in national marches on Washington. I've sued a property management company for discrimination after an eviction attempt when my lover moved into my one-bedroom apartment. I've come out to the mother who raised me. And we're fine. Why do I feel so anxious? The flip side begins playing. What's also true is that I've not come out to many people individually. Not to my father or brother or anyone else in my adoptive family. I just assume everyone who pays attention has figured it out. I rarely see them anyway.

Maybe it's like so much else that has been thrown up into the storm of 'where does all this really come from?' Am I really a McMahon or a Shields? Am I a product of a white, middle-class Chicago suburb, or a clan that seems to have been more transient and unsettled? Am I really gay? Is it in the genes? I surely am not straight, but even when living in San Francisco, I never really meshed with the gay community. It might be said that I've never really meshed with any community.

I flinch and stand. Time for a break. Time for a shower.

In the bathroom, I pause at the mirror. For just a moment, I see my face as if I were someone else looking at it. Objective, not connected to self-image, self-love, or self-loathing. It's outside, painted on a plane of glass, not melded with the person who has lived in this body for thirty-three years. It takes concentration to detach and see this face without preconception, without judgment. Who is this person? Who is he really?

With fresh clothes and the scent of Right Guard restoring order to my world, I sit back down, answer questions from her previous letter and conclude with, "Be in touch soon, Patrick." Yes, I like the double meaning. One, I will be in touch soon. Two, I've just told you I'm gay so I'll be in a heightened state of anxiety and irrational fear until I hear from you.

In a loopy state of relief and moxie, I address and seal the envelope, drive it to the post office, feel it slip from my fingers into the mailbox, and drive on to a Renaissance Fair where I can regress several centuries, duck below performing birds of prey, cheer on jousters, hurl axes into wooden targets, barbarically munch on mutton, and revel in the adolescent antics of a jester team called Puke & Snot.

THE TRUTH IS I'VE BEEN WORRIED ABOUT THIS FROM THE BEGINNING OF THE SEARCH OVER A YEAR AGO.

On a cold Tuesday in early November, my mailbox holds a folded 8 1/2 by 11 manila envelope. The return address label proclaims it's from ***Her***. Relief, joy, and anxiety accompany me up the stairs as I turn on the heat, peel off jacket and sweater, settle into the sheet-covered living room chair, and carefully slice open the envelope. It seems much longer than three weeks ago that I sent off my letter. Winter has begun since then.

Out slide the family trees I sent her, with handwritten additions. And then a letter. A very long letter. Sixteen handwritten pages on notebook paper.

She begins with news, then addresses some of the other questions I asked, and soon I'm noticing quite keenly that she's not mentioning the one radioactive paragraph from my letter, the one that's had me on pins and needles for three weeks. My mind has been taunting and terrifying me with ***What if she can't handle it?*** We haven't met yet, but things have been going well. What if she goes away? Again!

Finally, on page eight, she gets to it. *"I really haven't been avoiding your statement about the fact that you are gay. I have, I believe, saved the best for last. The fact that you had the courage to tell me this early made me feel very privileged. I can tell you this much, my dear, that doesn't affect my feelings in the slightest because I have always tried to be fair in how I treat others and hoped they would treat me the same way."*

As I drop the letter in my lap, a long exhale escapes. My whole body relaxes. My heart fills with relief. The truth is I've been worried about this from the beginning of the search over a year ago. My mother accepts me the way I am. She's not going to bolt. I find myself audibly sighing as a tear trickles down.

And then, I no longer care. I no longer care about all the worry, or what people might think if they saw this grown man reacting this way. Right now, I want to get in my truck and drive the 1600 miles to my first mother's house. I want to sit face to face so I can throw my arms around her and sob on her shoulder and tell her how much it means to me to hear these accepting words from my own flesh and blood. I want her to hold me as the tears wash away all resistance and allow this kid, this teenager, this young adult to be loved and accepted. I want her to love me, and I want to love her. In this moment, if I were a puppy, I'd be wiggling around on my back, getting petted and stroked. My eyes would glaze. My tongue would hang out. I'd be surrendering to the effects of a nirvana-inducing belly rub.

Patrick McMahon is an adoptee 18 years into reunion with his original family. He has written a memoir about his reunion, entitled *Becoming Patrick,* which he will be publishing in 2010. He lives in San Diego where he is also a photographer and musician. Find him at www.patrickmc.com.

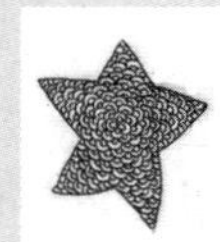

Waking Up American

By Jared Rehberg

I see you on my TV
Rushing home from work on crowded streets
You've got bills to pay and mouths to feed
I'm send you my prayer for another day

Without me, without you
I'm living in America with a brand new name
Without you, without me
I'm waking up American on a brand new day
And I'm still the same, I'm always the same

I think if you as I share good night
The answers to my questions wait by the light
So, what's my name? I think heaven sent
A moment of peace for God's creations

My country tis of thee, sweet land of liberty
For thee I sing, for thee I sing

I want to run with ghosts, across empty fields
I'll fish on the delta with the past by my side
Sometimes I wonder, what might have been
Choking on my destiny I found tears

Without me, without you
I'm living in America with a brand new name
Without you, without me
I'm waking up American on a brand new day
And I'm still the same, I'm always the same

I see you on my TV,
Rushing home from work on crowded streets

Jared Rehberg is a 34-year old Vietnamese adoptee from Northboro, MA.
His lyrics for "Waking Up American" is a dedication to his birthparents.

Dear Lucy (or any other adopted teen),

I loved you for thirteen months before I met you. But you didn't love me, because you didn't know that I even existed. That very first time I met you you looked into the eyes of a stranger, but it was through the eyes of a mother that I loved you the moment our eyes met.

Now, all these years later, we are together, our lives intertwined... I can't imagine my life without you in it, but I do reflect on that from time to time because you are adopted. I realize that you would have had a life without me. Spanish would have been your native tongue, and the sights, sounds, and tastes of life would have been very different, indeed, had you lived your life in Guatemala.

Does that mean your life would have been worse? Better? It's impossible to speculate, really, but I am sure it is something you've thought about quite often. In the darkness of the night when it's hard to get to sleep, do you think about what life would have been like in Guatemala with your birthmother? When you see images of extreme poverty, with children living on the streets or digging in trash dumps, do you sometimes wonder if that could have been your fate? Do you ever feel 'survivor's guilt'?

I'll don't know, just as you'll never know what life would have been like in your birth country.

As you become more and more your own person, please realize one thing—you are you because you are you. The experiences that shape our lives make us who we are, and that is constantly changing and evolving as we move through various life experiences. Love brought you into this world, and it brought you to me. I am honored to be the person that you call 'Mom.' My love for you knows no bounds; it is limitless and unconditional.

Make your life what you want to make of it. You don't owe the world anything except your God-given talents and your desire to make the world a better place. Celebrate who you are—share your strengths and passions—and by doing so, you will bring joy to everyone with whom you come into contact. Being adopted is not who you are, but it is a part of you. Don't magnify it and don't minimize it, but respect it and honor it for what it is and what it has brought to your life.

I am proud of you and the you who you've become. I look forward to getting to know the you who is evolving right before my eyes.

Love,
Mom

Amy Shore lives in Houston, TX with her husband Dave and their daughters Miranda and Lucy. She is an adoption counselor, author, and teacher–but 'Mom' is her favorite title!

A Bored Game

by Melanie Recoy

Did someone give you this book? Are they watching you right now? Are there about a million things you'd rather be doing than reading another book about adoption? Does the thought of discussing this book make you want to run screaming from the room? You are not alone. As an adoptee, I had these conversations more than I want to think about. Even if being adopted isn't a big thing to you, it is to your folks. Your adoption was what they would call a major life experience. It's just one of those things that you have to deal with. There is a talk in your future and you need some strategies to get through this as quickly and painlessly as possible. It will be best for both of you.

Step 1: Recognize the approach.

It's going to come sometime when they have you alone without an easily accessible route of escape. In the car, over lunch in a public place, possibly in a room where the only exit that can be effectively blocked by a faux casual leaning on the door frame. They'll have that look like they want to talk about something: the subtle tightening of the upper lip, a deepening of the lines in the forehead, you've come to recognize these things already. If you haven't committed any major infractions in the last few hours, you can bet it will be the dreaded adoption talk.

Show no indication that you saw it coming. Things will go much smoother if you let them feel that they are in control. Play along, give no hint of frustration. You want this over. Things could be worse, it's not the sex talk, after all.

Step 2: Let them get it out.

Remember this is important to them. Everybody wants to feel like they are doing well, parenting is no different. They aren't alright unless you are alright. Alright? Your life is going to roll easier if they think they have this handled. Your job is to instill a sense of confidence.

Let them say what they need to say. Just let them roll, make eye contact, do not turn your back; they will innately see this as a sign of aggression. Consider nodding when appropriate. Make mental notes of major points to address later in the Q and A session, which always follows. If you can get through this stage, you are halfway home.

Step 3: Restate.

At this point your parent has played his or her hand, you know what they need. Start addressing their concerns one by one, slowly. After each point allow them to respond. Keep things on message. Do not introduce new points or address anything not directly related to the issue at hand. Remember this is about them and instilling a feeling of confidence. Don't give them anymore to worry about. It's not a great time to mention that clown theme birthday party that didn't go so well, they remember, trust me.

Step 4: The Q and A session.

After you have addressed the issues, the parent will still need more clarification. At this point things can go terribly astray if not handled delicately.

More than likely you will hit on a point that you cannot clarify your position on to their understanding. First, try to repeat their position and move on to the next issue. Keep in mind if you don't keep things moving you risk prolonging this talk and future episodes focusing on this issue alone. Neither of you want that. You might consider conceding this point for the time being. It can always be revisited when you have come up with a clear strategy. Wars are almost never won on the strength of a single battle. The objective is to get through this talk alive.

Step 5: Summarize and Bail.

Repetition is good. It's the best way to end the dreaded Q and A session. Start listing the things that you have discussed. Keep it short and sweet. Do not embellish. Move over the stickier points quickly. End on a high note, something you were in complete agreement on. You can lay it on a little thick here, but don't get carried away. You don't want to raise their suspicions and lose all the ground that you have gained. Just let them know that you have heard what they said.

Now is the time to allow the parent to summarize. If things are on track, they will repeat what you just said. Again, repetition is good. Listen patiently. If they try to slip back into the Q and A, simply summarize again. This gives them the signal that the talk is coming to an end. Whatever you do, stay cool, it's almost over.

Step 6: Seal the deal.

By this time your parent should be feeling pretty good about themselves. Your goal has been achieved. Now change the subject. Pick something like dinner or the weather. You might consider going as far as asking them about a hobby or project they have been working on. It's up to you to judge their state of mind and if that would be too much. You can change back to half listening mode now. It's boring, but it sure beats adoption talk.

These strategies will hopefully help instill that confidence that every parent needs. They should also leave you with more time to do the things that you really want to do. I can't say you'll never have to have another adoption talk, but at least they may go smoother.

Step 7: Now glance up to see if you are still being observed. If so, give them your best cheesy grin.

Melanie Recoy is an adult domestic adoptee living in the Midwest. She is a writer, a weaver, and an adoptee rights activist.

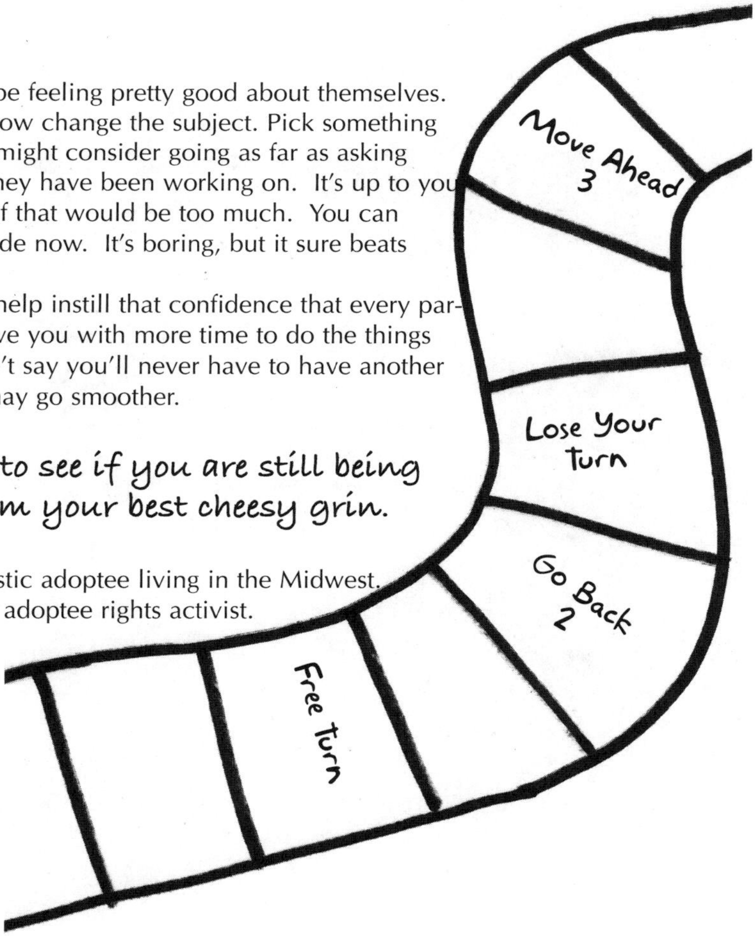

Move Ahead 3

Lose Your Turn

Go Back 2

Free Turn

Tag Cloud T-Shirt
by Jessica Emmett

I am a freelance Artist from the UK. I recently made this t-shirt as an example to some teens in an adoption art workshop I ran in Hong Kong with Jennifer Jue-Steuck. My t-shirt was very much influenced by Internet tag clouds. Why don't you try making one? Use permanent markers unless you want to change your words with each wash of your shirt.

I have been lucky enough to talk to many adoptees & adoptive parents. It seems that sometimes it's easy to forget that adopted "children" grow up, move away from home, get jobs, and have families of their own. I have always promoted that I am not only an "adoptee," but being adopted is only part of who I am. I am an artist first and for most of the time in my life even though adoption is the main theme in my art. Adoption, though, is not what defines me. I've always struggled with "labels," whether it be with ones others put on me or ones I choose for myself, mainly because I have never fit neatly into on category or another. Now I'm proud I am myself, with all my flaws.

For a great site to create electronic word clouds, visit www.wordle.net

Where Do These Pieces Go?

I'd like to say that like a real-life jigsaw puzzle, all of the pieces in your life will find a place. But that's not true. I won't lie. There are pieces of your life you just aren't sure what to do with.

That is what this section is about, those pieces we don't know what to do with. It's kind of like that mixed up piece in the box that doesn't fit or that piece you just can't figure out no matter how many ways you rotate it.

These pieces are on-going struggles of where to find healing or how to fit relationships into our lives. They are statements, songs, art, and stories about feeling out of place and feeling uncertain. They declare that we don't know what to do next. They capture those moments when we just don't know what to do.

In this section, you will find that your personal puzzle, your Pieces of Me, is a life-long journey. It is a journey where you find pieces and you fit them. It is a journey where you are continually searching for pieces. It is a journey where you discover there are some pieces you'll never get back. It is a journey where you constantly learn, grow, discover, and become more of who you are and who you want to be.

Enter the struggle with others as the moment unfolds. Recognize that their struggle is just like yours, trying to figure out this journey of life, sometimes knowing and sometimes not.

All of it okay.

Red Streak Of Blue Sky

Song Lyrics by Jasmine Renee Pyne

You don't who I am, You think I don't have a plan
You think I really can't, You put my head in the sand

I know who I am, I don't get your ways
You don't really know, You don't really care
You just want someone to scare

Maybe I'm an outsider, Maybe I don't fit in
Maybe I'm a red streak of blue sky

You think following is cool, You use mean as a tool
You think you always rule, You make people feel like a fool

I know who I am, I don't get your ways
You don't really know, You don't really care
You just want someone to scare

Maybe I'm an outsider, Maybe I don't fit in
Maybe I'm a red streak of blue sky

Maybe you like your ways, I don't know what to say
Have you ever looked back at the day
At the person you just talked to that way

Maybe I'm an outsider, Maybe I don't fit in
Maybe I'm a red streak of blue sky

 Another song by Jasmine can be found on page 69.

It's funny how growing up you never quite know why you have the experiences that you do, until you find yourself on an unusual path and realize you are right where you should be.

My Mixed Race Perspective

by Susan Crawford

I grew up in Kitchener, a city west of Toronto. My mom is Yugoslavian and of German descent, and my dad is black American and Choctaw Indian from Texas. We lived with my grandparents on my mom's side for eight years, which meant that I had lots of European influence growing up. I didn't have many chances to spend time with other black people when I was young since my dad's family all lived in the States, and I didn't have any friends whose families resembled mine.

Growing up, like most kids, I questioned who I was and where I belonged. Mixed race, multiracial, biracial, black...all these words only described a facet of who I was. But they became the focal point of my journey. What are you? Where are you from? Where are your parents from? Question after question, for as long as I can remember, made me memorize my racial/cultural makeup so I could quickly and easily answer the question and divert attention elsewhere.

I didn't want to be in the spotlight. I got a lot of attention from people growing up because of my Diana-Ross like hair and my ambiguous features. I had no idea why was it so important for someone to know where I came from, but soon figured it was because I was usually the only person who looked like me wherever we went. It was from the constant questioning and hair touching from strangers that I became very aware and self conscious of myself. I always knew that no matter where I went, because of my features, people would be staring at me. Whether they were or not, I always felt like I had a huge spotlight on me when I would have much preferred to blend into the background.

It was important for my parents for as long as I can remember to talk to us about race. These weren't always easy conversations to have, and looking back, I always perceived my dad to be really negative and melodramatic when recounting his stories because I didn't understand them or, I think more poignantly, didn't want to believe that they could be true.

Either way, the conversations were open and for my brother and I, the message was clear: work harder and be better because there were some people in the world who thought we were not as good as them because of the color of our skin. I didn't understand what this meant as a kid because I didn't 'see' myself as black. My dad was black. I was, well, in between. I couldn't understand why people would treat me differently because of how I looked. Were those members of my family who opposed my parents' marriage some of the people who would think less of me? Did they think less of my dad? Did my mom commit the worst offense in their eyes by marrying a black man? Would this affect what they thought of me? I had all of these questions but never had a clear answer.

As a teenager, I was always feeling like I was the only one who looked like me (black girl, big hair, white mother), had a family that was mixed in race and culture, and questioned where I belonged. I was constantly accused of being white washed, a sellout, or wannabe because I didn't act stereotypically "black," the way people thought a person who looked like me should be acting, this from both blacks and whites.

I was embarrassed when someone asked what my background was, knowing they were going to ask if I spoke German just to see if I was telling the truth. I would look at magazine covers and see the white faces of models with long blonde hair and slim bodies and would wish that I could look that beautiful. Why didn't pants fit my backside properly? Why doesn't my hair lay flat when I straighten it? And why can't I be as beautiful as they are? It was always clear to me that I was not 'desirable'– I looked different than the norm, my family was different because we didn't match, and all I wanted to do was blend in.

In a way, I have to admit, I was pretty successful at the blending in part. I would go to school and no one treated me differently (I thought), and I didn't see myself as any different from the people around me because I played the part well. It was only when my dad came to pick me up from school, or I let my big, curly hair down for the first time, or got braids that I would feel completely exposed. Like my cover had been blown and people would know that I was in fact...not white. What made these experiences harder was that while I was growing up, none of this made sense.

All of these revelations have come from lots of questioning and self reflection. I have come to the conclusion that I was scared of being different. More specifically, I was scared of being black – or at least what I thought it meant to be black. I removed myself so far from being a person of color that I did everything in my power to contradict it. I was ashamed of being different, I was embarrassed about looking the way I did, and more sadly, I felt like I was betraying my parents for feeling all these negative thoughts about myself. It was hard not to hate who I was if I looked around me– my community, my school, my friends and my extended family (because of geography) were all white. For someone trying to 'fit', it was impossible.

After graduating high school, I went to Wilfrid Laurier University. At university, I expanded my social circle considerably and took advantage of the opportunity to meet and interact with people from various cultures and races. My social circle started to include a close group of South Asian friends who called themselves 'brown'. There's a brown? I started experimenting with identities that I could fit with and thought that maybe I could be brown too! I figured out that it was sort of an exclusive label that I didn't fit under, and I still didn't have a category for myself. It was only when I applied to graduate school for a Social Work degree that I had the choice identify myself as a person of color. I checked the box that asked if I wanted to identify myself as a visible minority and thought, wow, I am 21 and just figured out I wasn't white. This was my turning point and the beginning of my journey of self discovery. I was scared, confused and embarrassed that at this age, I still didn't know who or what I was. But I checked the box. It was a start.

I moved to Toronto in 2001 and decided to conduct my research on mixed race youth. It was through the youth I interviewed that I finally felt as though I wasn't alone. Once I came to the realization that being different wasn't a bad thing I was able to look in the mirror and appreciate who I was. Being constantly submerged in a sea of white faces in every classroom, workplace and family gathering was never a challenge until I realized that I wasn't 'one of them'. I thought throughout my adolescence that I could blend in well enough that no one would notice that I was different. Different didn't get dates, different makes people stare, and different leaves you wondering what's wrong with you.

No one said that who you are today is who you have to be tomorrow. My identity has been fluid and ever-changing. One thing I noticed was that my search for self – who I am, where I fit, and who I wanted to be has never remained the same. Since I was 21 and really began to embrace my mixed race identity and explore what it meant, I find I am always asking questions and trying to learn more about myself. I, by no means have this figured out. There are still days I wonder where I fit, if I am good enough, or if people are looking at me because of my hair or because they like my shirt. I still second guess if the opportunities I have received in my life are because I worked hard for them or if I was just another token. I also still wonder if I am getting pulled over at the border because of a random check or because of the way I look. None of these questions I think will ever be answered.

What I have learned through all these experiences is that being comfortable in the skin you're in goes far beyond color, it is how you choose to portray yourself while navigating how others choose to categorize you. It's feeling confident about who you are, defining for yourself who you want to be. There are so many labels put on us based on our gender, age, color, religion, etc. that it's sometimes hard to break free of them. I find that when I stop trying to fit into someone else's definition of me that I am the happiest. Being mixed race has been a learning journey for me and my family, and it is something that I realize I should never have been ashamed of. Day by day I am learning how to be proud of my roots, who I am and where I came from. It hasn't always been easy to understand or accept, but it is what makes me who I am.

Being comfortable in the skin you're in goes far beyond color, it is how you choose to portray yourself while navigating how others choose to categorize you.

Susan Crawford is a graduate of the Social Work program at the University of Toronto. She grew up in a multiracial family and wrote a thesis on the identity of mixed race youth from a Canadian perspective. In 2007, Susan developed the Transracial Parenting Initiative, an educational training curriculum for families adopting and fostering children of a different race or culture. Susan is a 2009 recipient of the North American Council of Adoptable Children's (NACAC) Adoption Activist award.

dust to dust

by Juli Jeong Martin

he asked me what i knew about them
& naively i said, not much
two names, two ages, a place
vague intake about education & employment
extended family
just words
cold & distant
nonspecific

but he takes a beat & meets my eyes
that sounds to me like a lot, he says
& i feel his words before they reach my ears

something inside me shatters
with a shrill and tinny sound
because i know he's right.

where do you begin
when all you have
is a subway station

i guess that makes me lucky
or maybe
just less unfortunate.

i've been sitting, staring at these papers
the pages that should tell me who i am
but i can barely look in the mirror and see myself
much less the face of anyone else
so how can these words
form tangible realities
believe me, i've been looking
still i can't see if i have her eyes
i can't see her at all.

& today
it feels like nothing
because these papers aren't the answer
these words will tell me nothing more
than names and dates and places
i can't read between what isn't there
& find myself in empty words
these pages hold no secrets

where do you begin
when all you have
is a subway station

no, those are trapped by
shaded eyes & sealed lips
the mother-not-mother
wearing her baby under corset
she is the one in hiding.

& someday
maybe not so far away
when the need for answers
any answer
outweighs my fear
& the thought of never knowing
hurts more than painful truth
i will have a person to look for
i will have something to hold on to
somewhere to begin
not a street corner
park bench
or police station doorstep
but a name.

it's ironic that
the meticulous registries
the sacred bloodlines
always used to explain
my impossible being
might someday
lead me to her

but today
it feels like nothing

we are all chameleons
shape shifters dodging tracer bullets
reminders that we have been abandoned
we will bend & twist our bodies
so as to never be caught in a mirror's stare
our own reflections foreign meaning

all we'll never be
all we'll never see
& maybe that's why
i've chased escape
down many dark and lonely paths
because it catches up with you
not being able to meet the eyes
of your reflection

so i trace the lines along my body
like family trees without the names
perhaps someday i'll get it right
& learn to read them like a book
these papers i've been sitting
staring at for days
maybe they will bring
me someday to a face that i can recognize

but i can't wish for that
so today it feels like nothing
& these papers are just papers
these words are just words
they will not tell me anything
to make tomorrow easier
so i put them in their silence
away

maybe someday
not too far away
they will bring me comfort
lead me to the mother
& the answers that i seek
but today
they feel like nothing
& that woman
only carried me so far

before she walked away
there are others
who do not walk away
there are those who beat this path
with timid footsteps first
but now we walk a hundred wide
hand in hand
& sharing what we've learned

i'll never know
the person that i could have been
& i can't go home
again
if that home was never mine

but this, this i am a part of
& my blood is flowing
in time with poongmul drums
i feel the weight of what's been lost
& see the shape
of what was left behind.

--
Juli Jeong Martin

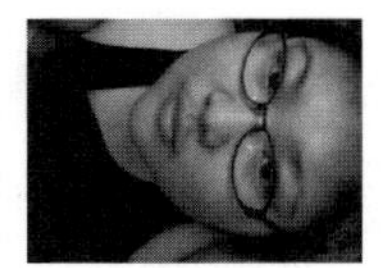

This reflects upon my journey within the adoptee community and how that has influenced the way I think about my past.

founder, editor
Grinding Up Stones:
The Asian Adoptee 'Zine
grindingupstones.wordpress.com
Find more of Juli's thoughts on pages 28, 47, 72, and 122.

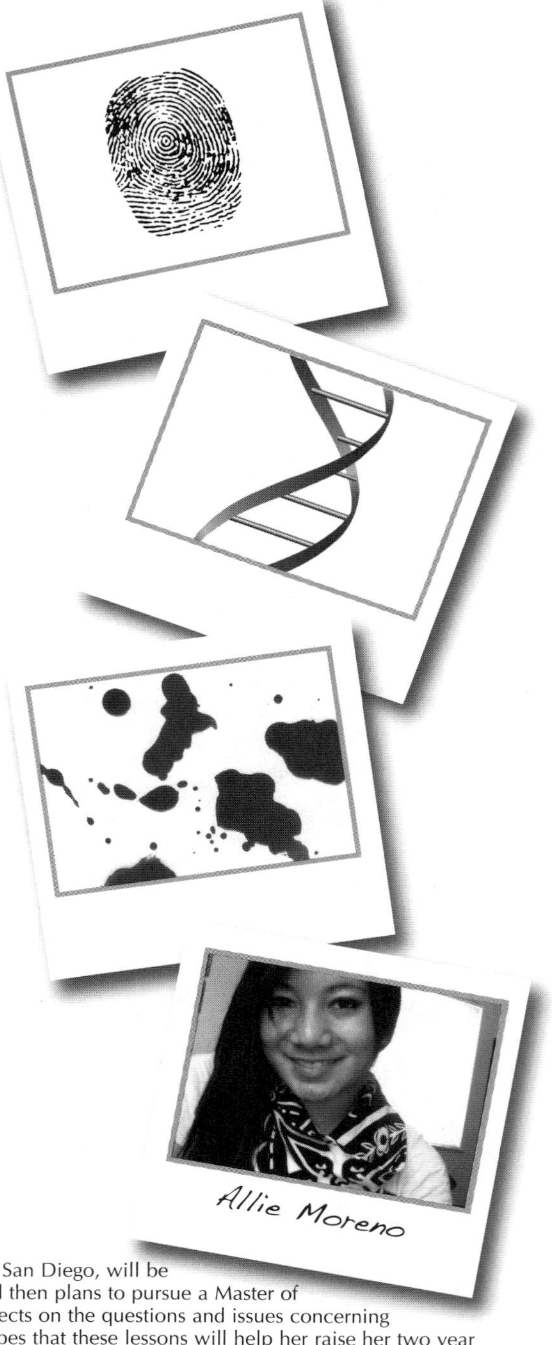

Polaroid Past

by Allie Moreno

a refugee of familial nests
I can't break free of the box
my mother left me in
nor let go of the envelope
where I keep her

victorious fear she left
me here abandoned to
be rescued though
a new identity
cannot erase a history

I carry remnants of a
polaroid past glazed
with whispered variations
of my ancestry

I often wonder
about my blood to whom
it belongs and where else
it runs—as recognizable as a
swan with a strawberry back

I imagine origins
dream the indigenous land
seeking the strangers
I long to know

Allie Moreno, a twenty-one year old adoptee from San Diego, will be graduating from Cal State San Marcos this year and then plans to pursue a Master of Fine Arts in Poetry. Her poem, "Polaroid Past", reflects on the questions and issues concerning cultural diversity within an adopted family. She hopes that these lessons will help her raise her two year old son to embrace both his culture and his family.

Running from Racism

by Heidi L. Adelsman

The Beginning

Before my older brother Mike started to run away from home at twelve years old, we lived and played like other American kids—or so I thought. Looking back, I've learned that the life our family lived was different from how most Midwestern American children grew up in the 1960s and 70s. As a racially mixed family, we experienced a contradiction of both racism and privilege.

As a racially mixed family, we experienced a contradiction of both racism and privilege.

When my brother was adopted he was 18 months old. He was in four foster homes before us. After he moved in, every single night for the first month he messed his pants. "What is home?" I could hear him say before he could talk. That first day Mom recalls that he wanted to be held by our dad, to sit in his lap only.

My parents chose to adopt because my mother, who was a social worker, saw too many African American children waiting to be adopted. Not long after he was adopted my parents divorced. This was the beginning of me seeing and feeling racism around us.

Our neighborhood was nearly all white. It was very intentionally this way. Like many communities across the United States, the houses in our neighborhood were built with racially restrictive covenants saying "Caucasians only." Racially restrictive covenants were banned in the late 1940s but it changed little.

Housing segregation led to a lawsuit that demanded equal education for all students in our city. White parents at my school who didn't want busing lobbied local politicians, our family friends and said there would be huge racial fights. I was told that on the first day of school all the white kids were going to be beat up by all the black kids. I was scared.

When my brother started to run away I thought it was all his problem. I couldn't understand what was happening to our family. But I don't remember him not being there. I don't want to remember him that way.

The Running

From ages twelve to eighteen Mike didn't live at home much. There were times he would return after treatment programs or from a detention center. It was expected that when he returned from a program he would be "fixed." But after a few times of him going away to be treated, it became like a game. "Go home and try to be better because we've doctored you in a different way." No amount of medicine or treatment could save him. The routine seemed so obviously ineffective. I felt hopeless. I either blamed my brother or said nothing.

There were no people of color in our lives and we felt disdain from the white community for race mixing as much as we tried to ignore it. My mom and our family were constantly harassed. Once, the radiator blew in our station wagon in the suburbs. Mom left the three of us in the car to go call her dad. Walking into any public facility with her three children, one blond, one brown and one black haired was a chance she couldn't take. In support of school desegregation, Mom lobbied at school meetings until someone in the audience jeered, "She's the one with the little nigger baby." After leaving for school one morning the same people called to say they saw her brown-skinned son at the bus stop. Another time they called her boyfriend to say his car was on fire, burning in the parking lot, and that Mom had been in a horrible car accident. Other times they called to say they knew where she'd been or threaten to break in our home. She was stalked and harassed. We didn't discuss the calls, but I remember them.

As my brother grew older, he ran further. He lived on the edges of America, in Los Angles, New York, and Key West. At times it seemed he was in search of a connection with an African American man, for the father he never knew. His white birth mother said of his birth father, "I loved him but I didn't know his name." Mike and I talked a few times a year, saying we missed each other, informing each other of our lives, and rehashing our past as I went through college.

The racism our family experienced is not common to most white folks.

The Wondering

At twenty eight years old, Mike died of AIDS-related lymphoma, a cancerous tumor. He had burned his face smoking a pipe and a tumor grew out of that scar, a scar that couldn't be contained with radiation. His teeth and jaw bones were melting. The doctors said, "There's nothing more we can do." We waited for the tumor to return, to watch him die before us.

Being raised with my brother and seeing him die at such a young age leads me to question if Mike's life have been different if he hadn't been through so many foster homes, if he had known his father or if our family didn't suffer the racism we lived with in south Minneapolis? As a teenager I didn't understand the impact racism had on our life. We didn't talk about it in school or at home.

Today, it is the lens that informs my view of life. The racism our family experienced is not common to most white folks. Many white people don't want to talk about it, denying that privilege and racism did and does exist. And that we can challenge it in part by not denying our past. Our city is still divided on the old race lines, the streets and avenues that define segregated housing patterns. The myth continues that unequivocally there's equal access to decent employment, housing and education for all. I now see the racism we experienced as a microcosm of American life, representing not just a problem within our family or community, but within our society and the world order we live in today.

"I have a dream that my four little children will one day live in a nation where they will not be judged by the color of their skin, but by the content of their character."

Martin Luther King, Jr.

Heidi L. Adelsman, shown here with her brother Mike, is a community historian who researches, speaks publically, and writes on housing and school desegregation and environmental justice issues. The other shot of Mike was taken when he was about 15.

LONGING FOR YOU

about Cindy (my birth mother)
Song lyrics by Lisa Douglass, an adopted teen

CHORUS

My life is empty without you,
I feel so lonely without you.
I don't know who I am
I've got a hole in my heart
Coz im missin you

BRIDGE

I long to know you
I'm seeking for you

V1

Are your eyes beautiful?
Does your hair flow down like a veil?
Just tell me the truth,
Why did you give me up?
CHORUS

V2

Do I wanna know you?
Do you wanna know me?
Are we gonna be?
Is it my destiny?
CHORUSx2

BRIDGEx3

Lisa Douglass was one of the teenage adoptees whose story is told in "The Girl in the Mirror." She wrote these lyrics about her birthmother. Lisa lives in Sydney, Australia.

How Do I Move Into the Light

How do I get through this darkness
Wanting to be alone
Feeling all alone
Wanting to scream
Only to sob
The aching, the fear
Of what is happening now
and what will happen next
Packing up the things I bought
for you
for us
brings new tears and new hurt
How did this happen
I was not supposed to be left
again
I am supposed to leave
later
When I am ready
When I am strong
I accepted the nothingness
of this relationship
I accepted the loss
of what I wanted
for the gains
that you received
I turn to the warmth of my dogs
but it's not the same
as two big hands
one big body
I want to smell you
I'm glad you took your clothes
I can't bear the scent
of loss
of abandonment
again

I wonder
if my mother cried
like I do now?
I wonder
if she still cries
No, no!
This is not about mother
But it is
All loss smells the same
Can't focus
Can't sit still
but can't move
I rock, like the infant I still am
He still calls
and I wonder

Is it better to be abandoned quickly or a little at a time?

I've experienced both
I think quicker is better
The cut heals faster
numbs quicker
but the scar remains
How do I move into the light?
What light?
The dog paws me for attention
Wags and licks as I pet
I am her light
For now, that will have to do

Find Eun Mi's other poems on pages 43, 53, 60, 73, and 121.

尹先生
Mr. Yin

by Jenna Cook

Riding home on the public bus together, Mr. Yin and I jerk with every frequent stop. "Zhong Han Lu, 到了!"—The bus's automated voice announces our arrival. Passengers' sweaty bodies slam against me in the process of escaping the standing crowd. Bewildered, I cling to my bag and hug close to Mr. Yin. "Hey! Watch it!" he yells in Chinese to a young man who elbowed me off balance. The man, intimidated by Mr. Yin's substantial build and authoritative stance murmurs, "Umm… 对不起 (Sorry)." Mr. Yin and I wait until he exits before jumping off of bus #803.

"华斯 (Jenna)," he calls, "What would you like to eat?" At only 4 p.m. he already contemplates dinner. The life of the Wuhan's people seems to center around food. Instead of "Hello!", they greet by saying,"你吃过吗? (Have you eaten?)"

"Watermelon!" I exclaim, the same answer I will give him every afternoon for the next two weeks. In exchange for room and board, I tutor Mr. Yin's daughter in English. We walk over to the watermelon man, who wears a straw hat like an upside-down cone. Big, juicy watermelons spill over the wooden rickshaw. China's summer heat causes sweat to drip down my nose and collect on my upper lip. Just the thought of a juicy watermelon lures me. Carefully knocking each watermelon, Mr. Yin chooses a lopsided one "How about this one?" I suggest, pointing to a flawless, green melon. "不行, (It won't do)," he says. "The ugly ones always taste better."

He lugs the massive melon up the eight flights of stairs to his family's apartment. I tag behind, just a temporary visitor in his home. Mr. Yin teaches me to remove my dirty shoes, which have been walking on streets scattered with dark spots of urine and phlegm. He hands me a pair of clean and comfy slippers to wear instead.

"Tuoxie," he speaks Chinese slowly to make sure I understand. "Inside, we wear tuoxie."

The ugly melon's perfect juices, crisp with succulent flavor, drip down my chin. As I write in my journal and move to cross my legs, a picture falls out. "那是什么? What's that?" Mr. Yin asks. I hand him the picture of a young Chinese lady standing next to my adoptive Caucasian mother. "Have you seen this lady?" I ask in mangled Chinese. "I'm looking for my foster mother." Mr. Yin stares at the picture for a long time. Dawned in crisply ironed trousers and a freshly starched polo, the successful businessman seems to breathe opulence. His coarse black hair, just beginning to turn grey, stands alert on his head. Bold between his two eyebrows, his forebrow shines with Wuhan, China's sweat.

"She looks familiar," he says, commenting on the picture of my foster mother. "She looks so familiar." Mr. Yin's wife, Mrs. Zhang, and his daughter, Lily, gather around the picture.

"I want to find her," I say, looking directly into Mr. Yin's pupils. My gaze drifts to the high bridge of his nose and then back up towards his eyes. Then suddenly I realize, "Your eyelids!"

"I know," he says, unsurprised. "They're just like yours." The presence of his daughter and wife melts from my consciousness. How long ago had he noticed this? "We have the same," he says, pointing to his own eyes. I examine his complexion again, perplexed at the left eye with a lid and a right one without. "Do you know anyone else with eyelids like this?" he questions me.

"No. 不认识. I don't know anyone else."

That night when I brush my teeth at Mr. Yin's sink I examine my eyelids. With each swish-swish of the brush, my face seems to drift closer to the mirror. Scrutinizing my own appearance, searching for answers to my Chinese family, my forebrow suddenly morphs to become more pronounced like Mr. Yin's, my face rounder, the skin darker…

Lying awake in bed at Mr. Yin's house, I secretly dream Mr. Yin and I share the same blood. My finger twirls strands of slippery black hair, while I wonder what it feels like to say, "我爸爸 (my father)." Do Mr. and Mrs. Yin have secrets? I dare to question. Perhaps 14-year-old Lily was not truly their first daughter? Tugging on my Old Navy "made in China" nightgown, I turn onto my side, the bed's wooden boards digging into my ribs. "Mrs. Zhang could have given-up the first girl in the hopes of later conceiving a boy…" I play with the idea, rolling it round and tangling it up in my hair, in my fingers, letting it wash over my brain and seep into my heart. I remember the proud look on Mr. Yin's face, watching me teach English to concierges at his work just that day. It was almost… as if… as if I were his own daughter—

It was almost... as if... as if I were his own daughter—

Laughing from the hallway interrupts my thoughts. I tiptoe in my purple tuoxie to peak out the bedroom door. Hands hanging comfortably by my side, I peek through the crack in the open doorway. The family watches something I can't understand on the TV. Lily laughs at some swiftly spoken phrase as Mrs. Zhang combs Lily's hair into beautiful braids. Mr. Yin irons his tan trousers while smoking a gold-banded cigarette. He laughs with his wife and only daughter. His only daughter.

My hands retreat to the concave of my underarms. The tousled, black hair piled on my head seems plain compared to Lily's and the lingering sweetness of the watermelon doesn't taste as luscious as before. I miss the cozy embrace of my mother's white arms, the high-pitched voice of my little sister waking me up in the morning, the tones of a language I understand without pause. Alone in Wuhan, I scavenge for my Chinese roots, but in doing so leave behind the only family I now have. My eyes start to tear, and I retreat to the bed, burying my face in the familiar scent of my American pillow.

Jenna Cook is adopted from China and is a senior at Phillips Exeter Academy in Exeter, NH. She enjoys playing American folk music on her acoustic guitar and Chinese folk music on her Guzheng.

The Girl at the Window by Stacy K. Pearson

'Girl at the Window' depicts the reflections on life and who you are that sneak into the little moments of an adopted person's world. On the original image, the girl has a number of different colors on her that represent the different feelings, questions, and emotions that adoption brings. It is also those things that set those who have been adopted apart from people who have not experienced it.

Find Stacy's other art on pages 9, 18, 49, 52, and 101.

How I'll Remain...

By Xiu Xiu Cooney

How I'll remain in pain is a secret
A secret love that never can be told
As each day grows old

I realize that I've been hurt by you
More than once and more than twice
As I keep trying to roll the dice

I can never win
I always lose to you
Because I've always given in to you

You treat me as if I have no feelings
And you walk all over me
But you still can't see

I try to keep telling myself that it will be
over soon
Over and over
But when will that day ever come?

The answer is never,
Because this is how I'll remain
In this same secret sorrow pain.

Find Xiu Xiu's other writing on page 129.

Copy this page (especially if this is a library book!)

Using this page, write down these three things:

- Author/artist/person you most related to in the book. Why?
- Author/artist/person that impacted you the most. Why?
- Author/artist/person that didn't make sense to you. Why is that?
- What, if anything, are you going to do next to figure out your own pieces?

Share your thoughts on the Pieces of Me Who Do I Want to Be Facebook Group. See you there.....

Let It Go

By Chick Moorman

A teacher that I know did a very interesting activity.
Grab several sheets of toilet paper and a pen. (Markers work best on this paper.)

Write about something on the paper that really bugs you. Maybe it is an event that happened you would rather forget. Perhaps you told off a girlfriend or boyfriend when you were really thinking of something else. Maybe you were mean to someone or disrespectful. Maybe something didn't turn out as you had planned. Maybe it is something that happened to you that you didn't want to happen. Take a minute and record something that is bugging you on this wonderful, special paper.

Now, take what you have written into the bathroom. Open the lid of the toilet, toss in your paper with the stuff that is bugging you on it and pull the handle. That's right, flush that baby down the toilet. It's nice to let go of what is bugging you....

What's done is done. Let it go.

Get rid of bad feelings.

Writing it down and throwing it away helps you get rid of it.

Don't hang on to negative thoughts.

This is a mind skill that can be carried out physically, using the toilet, or you can use a mental flush.

Symbolic gestures and imagery help mind skills stick in the consciousness. The symbolism of actually flushing bad memories and what they represent down the toilet are right-brain activities. That's the stuff of long-term memory. So bury your "I can'ts." Flush your concerns, let it go and get on with your life.

Chick Moorman is the author of *Spirit Whisperers: Teachers Who Nourish a Child's Spirit*. He is one of the world's foremost authorities on raising responsible, caring, confident children. Find him at www.chickmoorman.com

Precious Jade 宝玉

by Jenna Cook

Two hours into an adoption presentation at Barcelona's Casa Asia, one parent who has adopted a young Chinese daughter asks me, "So, when are you going back to China?" I wait patiently while the question makes its way through the interpreter. I carry my US passport around my neck at all times when traveling. I carry a bottle of water in case my throat gets sore from speaking.

"I've returned in 2002 as well as 2006," I explain, directing my voice into the microphone, "both times with my Caucasian adoptive family. I plan to return this summer, by myself, to volunteer teaching English in my orphanage to thank the workers for the good care they took of me." Amidst the audience of sixty or seventy adoptive parents, I notice a middle-aged woman in the second row suddenly sit up in her chair. She listens intently.

"So, I am thinking about adopting another orphan from China," another parent begins. "What has been your experience with siblings? Is it something you would recommend?" I carry my experiences to share, like origami paper in my pockets. Traveling to talks, I know how to pick out the right pieces—blue for racism, red for culture, green for identity. I can fold the colored squares using just the right words and give the parents a crane, an orchid—some shapely advice out of my sheets of memories. I continue to answer questions, using my words to create the right folds. That lady in the second row never takes her eyes off me.

After the formal talk, the lady approaches me from the audience. A Spaniard who carries a tan leather purse. She wears glasses. Hair pinned in a bun. Simply dressed. Maybe forty. "Me llamo Yolanda," she says. And she then chokes and sobs. I feel my own lungs take on the pace of her breathing in that moment. Although I cannot speak Spanish, I sense how she stresses her words genuinely, thankfully, desperately. It makes me shake with tears, even before I know what the words actually mean. The translator is firm with her. "Speak to me first," she says, "Then, I will tell the girl."

"I bought three jade necklaces in a shop," Yolanda tells the translator, but she doesn't take her eyes off me. We stand close. "One for me. One for my Chinese baby daughter, the one I am waiting for. And one for someone else. I didn't know who I would give it to, but God told me to wear it here. And He was right." She unties a jade pendant from around her neck and then reties it around mine. "I know this is meant to be yours."

I stare down at the necklace, as one of my tears drops down to the floor. The delicate carvings and milky hues of the jade.

"When you go to China to work in the orphanage perhaps you will take care of my daughter."

The precious stone feels smooth and comforting and mysterious. I wrap my fingers around the coolness. I carry Yolanda in the jade. I carry her faith in me, in my work in the orphanage. I carry pride in my Chinese culture. The oriental design. I carry an adoptive mother's love. Around my neck. In my pocket. Near my heart. In my purse.

"Yolanda. Yolanda," I repeat to myself, feeling the roll of my own tongue. Of all the baby orphans in China, in all thirty-four provinces, I plan to go to only one orphanage—my own. The chances of me working with Yolanda's baby-to-be are near impossible, but clutching the jade in my palm, I know I will see Yolanda's baby in every orphan's face. I carry a new sense of purpose.

She hugs me for a long time after tying the necklace around my neck. Her arms wrap comfortably around my shoulders, sheltering me from the cameras and flashing lights of the adoption conference. In Yolanda's embrace I feel her immense longing for a child. A child she has never even seen or heard or touched. I witness a love that is as valid as a birth mother's love, as passionate and unconditional. I imagine the baby growing inside her—not inside her stomach, but inside her heart.

She tells me she has been waiting for two years already.

That night in bed I pray for Yolanda's baby. The jade, resting on my chest in the dark, moves up and down with my breathing. I run my fingers around the smooth curve of the jade – at the bottom a pear which curves seamlessly into a salamander. The salamander's body is camouflaged to look like the pear's leaf. The animal's face peeks from around the top—smiling and hidden.

"When you go to China to work in the orphanage perhaps you will take care of my daughter."

The necklace makes me want to pray. More than a church or monk or mosque. Because it found its way to me by some act of faith. Because she bought three necklaces for only a mother and daughter. Because at these conferences I speak of my adoption story as if I have stopped living it. And the truth is I don't know where life will take me. Because in that necklace I carry both of my mothers. Because someday maybe I hope I will fall into my Chinese mother's arms just as that necklace fell into mine.

On the way home to Boston, I carry euros and pounds and my native dollars, maps, metro receipts, and customs declarations. I carry my only souvenir—the green and glistening pendant—something I couldn't buy or shop for. I look into the eyes of the jade salamander perching on the pear, and think of Yolanda, and all of the mothers like her, who are waiting for children like me.

Jenna Cook is adopted from China and is a senior at Phillips Exeter Academy in Exeter, NH. She enjoys playing American folk music on her acoustic guitar and Chinese folk music on her Guzheng.

"I Don't Know"

by Cindy (Champnella) Koenigsknecht

I thought I was prepared for the teen years. After all, I'd been through them before with my oldest daughter, Kate. But nothing prepared me for the rite of passage that began for Jaclyn when she started middle school. Jaclyn, who was adopted at the age of four from China into a Caucasian family, has forever changed the way I see this world. What I've learned about race, from her, through her, because of her, have been the biggest lessons of all. But I was still taken aback when she came home from school one day, looked me in the eye and announced emphatically; "Oh, by the way, I am not going to marry anyone white!"

"OK," I replied, trying hard to keep my reaction neutral.

"Well, I just wanted you to know," she said, carefully searching my face.

Later in the week, she was invited to the birthday party of a classmate. The event was to be held in the party room of a local bowling alley. A few days beforehand she sidled over to me and very casually said, "Oh, by the way, when we go to Julie's party I want you to just drop me off in the parking lot. Don't come inside with me."

So I readily agreed to remain in the car, slowing the vehicle only enough to allow her to gently roll out the car door while I crouched behind the steering wheel, hidden from the view of her friends.

When we arrived the parking lot was practically empty. Jaclyn panicked, worried that maybe we had gotten the time or place wrong and then asked me if I'd walk in with her, just to be sure. As we made our way down the bowling alley hallway, one of her friends popped out of a room and, relieved, Jaclyn sprinted toward the door without even a backward glance. I was just a short distance away and could see Julie's mom standing outside the party room so I walked to her and introduced myself while peeking in the party room. My quick scan made a mental note of the fact that within the gaggle of party goers there was not a single Caucasian face.

I came to pick her up at the appointed time and Jaclyn was on high alert for my arrival. She spotted me when I was barely out of the foyer area, took off running with a shouted "good bye" to her friends and then ran by me, without a glance in my direction, as if she had no idea who I was, and hopped into the back seat.

I could not keep my silence. There was no way I could see to ease into this conversation. "Jaclyn, were you embarrassed to be seen with me because I'm white?" I said matter-of-factly.

"NO!" she exclaimed immediately. "Honestly, mom, you are so racist!" I was stung by the word as I take great pride in my love for all people and wondered for a moment if this hot denial meant I had struck too close to a truth. A few moments of silence elapsed. Then, so quietly that I almost missed it, she said; "Now all my new friends will know I'm adopted."

I Don't Know

I had no words for this. I thought she was ashamed of me when the truth is that she—the one I am most proud of in this world, the one who showed me that even a heart that has been broken can love hugely, the one who has every reason to think this world is an ugly place but embraces it instead with joy and resilience, the one who taught me what it is to live with a grateful heart—*she is ashamed of herself.* The words sit between us for days as it takes time before I can broach this topic again. This is too important. I need to not make a mistake this time; I have a long trail of mistakes made in parenting her already.

I consult with those who know more about adoption issues than I do and, when the time seems right, I broach this topic with her again. "Jaclyn, are you ashamed that you are adopted?"

"I don't know," she says evenly.

"You know that it wasn't your fault that your mom couldn't take care of you, don't you?" I say.

"I don't know," she replies.

"Is this about feeling different than your friends?"

"I don't know," she states flatly.

"You know that lots of people are adopted, right? It's just a different way to make a family—there is no embarrassment in it."

"I don't know," she says firmly.

"Can you tell me more about your feelings?" I say, almost pleading with her now.

"I don't know," she says with resignation. And then she meets my gaze and says simply: *"I just don't know what my feelings are."*

"I don't know," she says with resignation. And then she meets my gaze and says simply: "I just don't know what my feelings are."

She is being honest. As honest as she knows how to be. The not knowing is part of her journey.

Cindy (Champnella) Koenigsknecht, PhD, is an adoption advocate residing in Farmington Hills, MI. She is the author of; *The Waiting Child: How the Faith and Love of One Orphan Saved the Life of Another* (St. Martin's Press) and a feature writer for *Adoption Today* magazine. She is the proud mother of 3 daughters; two are Chinese adoptees.

Pieces of Me, Who Do I Want to Be? Puzzles

Directions

1) Make a copy of the puzzle on the next page and glue it to cardstock, foamcore, or some material that will stiffen the paper and make the pieces interlock better. If you don't have that, you can just use it as is. You can also use a blank puzzle, available in craft stores or online. (But who wants to wait to do this?)

2) Cut the puzzle pieces apart and write one thing that makes you who you are on the back of each puzzle piece. Make sure to write "Adopted from _______" or "Foster Care Alumni" on one of your pieces. (If you are using just paper, keep it together for this step, just hold it up to a window or light to put the things you want in the right spots.)

3) When you have finished that, put your puzzle back together.

4) Now draw a picture on the front of the puzzle that somehow represents you. Make sure that the picture you create touches each piece of the puzzle.

5) Think about how the puzzle is representative of you. Is there someone you want to share the image you made with?

6) Now take out the piece of your puzzle that is the "least important" in your picture. Is it still possible to tell what your picture is without that piece?

7) Take a look at the characteristic on the back of the puzzle piece. Would you still be who you are without that attribute?

8) Replace the "least important" piece of your puzzle.

9) Now Repeat steps 6 – 8 with the "most important" piece of your puzzle.

It's interesting to see that we are each made up of many pieces and not defined by just one of our pieces or attributes. Our "whole picture" is the sum of many parts. Some of our attributes are more central to our identity but may change over time as we age and have different experiences. Each of those pieces comes together in a distinctive way that makes each of us special and unique.

There is no one out there just like you!

The Journey is only Beginning

by Sarah Ballard

My name is Sarah. I'm not an adoptee, but I married one. In fact, I married the editor of the book you're holding, but you probably figured that out given we have the same last name.

Believe it or not, we've been married ten years now. We have two biological daughters and are adopting a son from Vietnam.

But Bert isn't my first exposure to adoption. I actually grew up with one brother and three sisters who were adopted from Korea. And I was also a counselor for a while and worked with adoptees and their families. To say that adoption is important to Bert and me is an understatement! Just because we write about it or earn a living from it, doesn't mean it has been easy for us. Especially because Bert is adopted himself (if you haven't yet, read the introduction to find out more about him).

This book uses the idea of puzzle pieces as a way to think about how we figure out who we are. It is about gathering pieces of ourselves we need to connect with. It is about the pieces that have been stolen from us. It is about fitting the pieces together to figure out who we are and who we want to be. It is about sharing our pieces and ourselves with the world. And it is about pieces that we are still trying to figure out.

Now you may think that because Bert has a "PhD" and has put this book together that he's got all his pieces figured out. You couldn't be further from the truth. In fact, in the time it has taken to put this book together, he has gone through each and every one of these puzzle pieces aspects of life.

For gathering pieces, Bert has gotten in touch with an adoptee friend of his he met a decade ago and they are forming a good friendship. It has been neat to watch them re-connect and share how they've grown and are different than they used to be. Yet they still have the common connection of being adoptees.

For stolen pieces, Bert is still coming to terms with what it means to have been separated from his birthmother. Even in his mid-thirties, married to a hottie (me!), and with two wonderful children, he still fears being rejected. Whether it is a friend who doesn't respond to an email or on Facebook or even when I don't respond to something he says, it taps into that deep wound of whether he will be rejected again – or more specifically, when he will be rejected again.

At the same time, for fitting pieces, Bert is beginning to accept how this fear of rejection plays out in his life, how he can use it to improve himself and those around him, and how he can reach out to other adoptees – like yourself! He's always finding ways to transform his pain and struggle into something positive for his life and for others.

For sharing the pieces, this book represents one way Bert has shared himself with others. But, Bert is much more than "just an adoptee." He likes to say, **"I used to be adopted, now I'm just me,"** a phrase one of his adoptee friends came up with. It means that there is more to who he is – and who you are – than just being adopted. Bert is a husband, a father, a teacher, a writer, and is learning to enjoy hockey! He likes to play Wii and stay up late and take late afternoon naps. He likes to travel to new places and reads lots of books he never finishes. Bert is so much more than "just an adoptee" – that's what I love about him. His being adopted gives him depth, but it's not the only thing you find when he shares who he is.

And for pieces he doesn't know what to do with, there are times Bert is still figuring out where the pieces of him go. His fear of rejection, his quest to love himself, his need for positive feedback – they raise their ugly heads when he least expects it. It wears him down. It throws him off and can even interfere in the good times. Sometimes he'll tell me, "I'm tired of being an adoptee." He doesn't mean it literally. He just means it's hard.

Picturing life in the form of puzzle pieces is appropriate not just for this book, but for Bert. Bert, like all of you, has lots of pieces to who he is. Bert gathers them, has some stolen, fits them, shares them, and sometimes doesn't know what to do with them. He's on the same journey you are.

And that is a good thing. No, that is the best thing.

Putting the Pieces of Me together is not a simple task. I wish it were. I wish it was as easy as pulling the puzzle out of the closet, dumping the pieces out of the box, and spending some focused time transforming the pieces into the picture on the cover. But there's no box to look at, and every time you think you have the puzzle together you find another piece, or another missing piece. Not to mention that the picture itself is constantly changing!

Anyone who does puzzles knows a good puzzle takes time. (I LOVE puzzles by the way! Maybe that's part of why Bert intrigues me so!) A good puzzle is not completed in one sitting. It's completed over time. You make good progress when you spend some focused time on it and then go away and come back. You make progress when you are walking by and a piece catches your eye that you never saw before. You make progress when you ask others for help. You make progress when you aren't looking to make progress!

That's how life is too. That's how figuring out who you are is. It's a journey. It takes time. Sometimes you really need to focus on yourself. Other times things will click and you won't know why. Other times you need to ask for help. Other times things will fit when you're not even looking to put them together. And some times, things will never fit, no matter how hard you try.

What you hold in your hand does not give you the answers to the *Pieces of Me: Who do I want to be?* What you hold in your hand is a collective starting point. This means that every person in this book and every other person reading it, each voice, is on the same journey you are. They are trying to gather their pieces, deal with their stolen pieces, fit their pieces, share their pieces, and struggle with where their pieces belong. Just like Bert. Just like you.

But this a wonderful journey. One you are not on alone. One that many are experiencing with you at the same time. This book is a beginning, a place where you can hear and read and understand what others are going through. A place where you can figure it out for yourself. And, we know you will. We know you will figure out the Pieces of Me and most importantly, you will figure out ***Who do I want to be!***

Ways to Connect

By Sarah Ballard

After reading all (or more than likely some) of this book, you're probably wondering, what next? There are a lot of ways you can connect with other adoptees and foster alumni as you continue to figure out the *Pieces of Me: Who Do I Want to Be?*

Consider the following:

1. Online Forums and Groups Online you will find organizations across the globe who are focused on connecting adoptees with each other. Some are specific to a certain type of adoption (area of origin or type) and some are more broad to include all adoptees. Most of these groups have online forums or email listservs where you can connect with other adoptees. A lot of them also have annual conferences or gatherings where you can get together in person. You'll want to ask your parents' permission, of course, before connecting with people online.

Groups.yahoo.com offers a great searchable database of groups with individual themes. Search by the topic you are interested in chatting or learning more about. **FosterClub.com** provides online networking. It also offers the opportunity for you to apply to become an All-Star. All-Stars travel the country inspiring younger peers and providing a youth's perspective into the child welfare system. **Adoption.com** has a forum area with a variety of sections covering open/closed domestic and international adoption. They also have a place you can register your information and search **registry.adoption.com** and look for birth family (you have to be 18 to post your information). **Experienceproject.com** has forums where you can post and chat anonymously about any life experience. **Heyjosh.com** offers practical teen insight that is direct and on your side and, oh yeah, he was a foster to adopt kid. **Fostercarealumni.org** is a place to connect if you are an alumni of the foster care system and they have resources to help you advocate to transform policy and practice for kids still in care.

Some tips when online. First, if you're under 18, make sure you have your parents permission, and don't disclose anything too personal that might allow someone unsafe to find you– be safe online. Also remember that what you post never goes away. Be conscious of what you share. Second, you can easily jump on Google or Yahoo and search for what you're looking for. If you want to find other teen adoptees, type in "teen adoptees." You want to find out more about transracial adoption, type in "transracial adoption." Curious about birth records, simply type in "birth records" and see what you find. You know how to do this! The most important thing is finding something that meets your needs and desires where you are in your own search. Trust me, there are unlimited resources out there – find the ones that work best for you!

2. Blogs Search for "Adoptee Blogs" to be able to read more stories and connect with others who have experiences like yours. Some bloggers have been continually blogging for a number of years while others come and go. You will find a whole host of different views as you click links to find voices that entertain, enlighten, and perhaps even entice you to try your hand at it as well.

3. Culture Camps There are several groups who hold culture camps over the summer months where adoptive families can come for several days and connect with other adoptive families. This is a great opportunity for you to meet other adoptees and spend extended time connecting with others like you before returning to everyday life (hopefully with new friends to text, IM, email, call, and plans to visit). There are also overnight camps that are adoptee only. A lot of these camps also enlist the services of teens as camp counselors for younger adoptees. You get to meet other adopted teens who are counselors AND have the opportunity to influence the minds of younger adoptees! Check out these sites: **www.heritage-camps.org**, **www.catalystfoundation.org**, **www.handsaroundtheworld.com**, **www.pactadopt.org**, **www.holtintl.org/camp** or do a search for "culture camps" or "adoption camps."

4. Homeland Tours If you started life in another country, there are places that offer homeland tours that can be with parents or without. They can help arrange for translators (if needed) and offer a group of like minded travellers to share your journey. For over 15 years, the Ties Program offers trips to a variety of countries – **www.adoptivefamilytravel.com**. Some agencies put together trips for adoptees who were adopted through their programs, so check with your agency to see if there are any available. There is a great listing for adoptees from Korea at **www.kaanet.com**. If you were adopted from China, there are groups who specialize in tours to China, **www.ocdf.org**, **www.lotustours.net**, or **www.alwaysforever.us**. Google "homeland tours (your country) adoption" to find links to specific tours.

5. Mentors A lot of teens I know have really connected with older/adult adoptees or foster alumni. It can be nice sometimes to talk to an adult who knows what it was like to be in your shoes and can relate to all of your feelings (happy, sad, angry, bitter, frustrated, joyful, and so on). You can contact an internet group or an adoption agency near you to see if they know of a local mentorship program or any older adoptees in your area who would like to hang out with a fun and interesting teen. You can connect with these kinds of people online too, if you can't find anyone near by where you live. Again, if you're under 18, be sure to get your parents permission and be safe.

6. Other Adoptive/Foster Families If your parents know of any other families in your area who also have adopted kids, you can ask them if you can get together with them for dinner every once in a while. I have met families who get together with several other families once a month just to connect. It can be nice for your parents to find other people who understand what their experience is like too! One great way to connect with other adoptive/foster families is through online listservs (see #1 above). Find a listserv, introduce yourself, and ask if anyone knows of any families near you that would like to get together. You might also ask your parent(s) or social worker if there are any families in your area who might be open to this kind of connection.

7. Counseling/Therapy Groups Counseling is another way to connect with others. You can find out if there are any adoptee-only or foster-only support groups in your area and join one. If there aren't any, find a counselor who knows something about adoption and ask them to start one. You don't have to have "problems" for a counseling group to be worth looking into. Just wanting to connect with other people who are like you is reason enough! If you do find that issues around being adopted overwhelm you or keep you from feeling like you are enjoying life, or even just burden you a little too much, one-on-one counseling can help, too. Finding a counselor who is adopted or who has a lot of experience with adoption can also really help you understand